TEAM DEVELOPMENT MANUAL
Second edition

Mike Woodcock

Gower

Published by
Gower Publishing Company Limited,
Gower House,
Croft Road,
Aldershot,
Hants GU11 3HR,
England

Gower Publishing Company,
Old Post Road,
Brookfield,
Vermont 05036,
USA

Reprinted, 1989

British Library Cataloguing in Publication Data

Woodcock, Mike
    Team development manual.—2nd ed.
    1. Organizations. Teams. Management —
    Manuals
    I. Title
    658.4'02

ISBN 0–566–02790–9

Printed and bound in Great Britain by
Billing & Sons Ltd, Worcester

TEAM DEVELOPMENT MANUAL

Second edition

For James and Victoria

Contents

Preface

Organizations are about people working together and, therefore, developing effective teams must be a prime responsibility of all who manage or lead groups of people. Although library shelves abound with volumes about the theory of management, little is available in the way of practical help to those who have the responsibility of leading and developing people in teams. This manual and its companion volume *50 Activities for Teambuilding* is an attempt to provide that help. This manual gives guidance about how teams can be made more effective, and *50 Activities for Teambuilding* presents a range of practical activities which can be used in organizations to bring this about. Together they provide many well-tried activities and techniques as well as explaining the essentials of team development. The manual also gives guidance on where to obtain further ideas and help.

Since its first publication in 1979 *Team Development Manual* has been used by thousands of managers to improve team functioning. This revised and expanded second edition incorporates much additional material. Throughout, my aim has been to keep each section as short and simple as possible for the benefit of busy people who want practical help rather than elaborate theory. I have used all of the material presented in organizational teambuilding assignments, in workshops, on seminars and in other teambuilding sessions or in my own businesses. The teambuilding events in which the material has been used range from directors' meetings to evening seminars, from in-company formal training events to residential workshops and from one-to-one coaching sessions to national conferences involving hundreds of people. Margarine manufacturers, electronics engineers, builders, bakers, mechanical engineers, accountants, consultants, brewers, company directors, wholesalers, retailers, magistrates, secretaries, training officers, milk processors, general managers, supervisors, clerks and many more have joined in the activities and helped to improve many of them.

I hope the manual will have a variety of uses. It can simply be read to give a grasp of teamwork concepts or it can be utilized as a source of ideas for anyone wishing to undertake practical teambuilding activities, or together with *50 Activities for Teambuilding* it can be used as a complete approach to organizational teambuilding programmes. To the manager it should be a source of practical ideas to implement in his or her own organization, to the student a source of theory and experiment, and to the skilled facilitator a source of further ideas and developmental activities.

THE LAYOUT

The decision to call this work a manual was of great importance: its success will not be determined by the number of copies sold, nor by the number of people who read it. It will be successful if it leads people to take action, to translate theory into practice in their own organizations, businesses, clubs or groups. Because of that I have laid out the material in a way which will enable it to be readily available for practical use.

Part I is about how to improve team performance. In eight separate sections it clarifies understanding of the principal characteristics of effective work teams and how they develop; considers the role of the team leader; gives guidance on action planning; presents a set of groundrules for team development; outlines the limitations of team-building; and suggests ways of designing teambuilding events.

Part II provides a unique instrument which helps to establish the development needs of teams.

Part III contains an explanation of the 'building blocks' of effective teamwork. Each explanation is in the form of a short lecture which can be used as a basis for input to training events.

Part IV provides a link between this manual and its companion volume *50 Activities for Teambuilding* (see below) by relating teambuilding activities to the building blocks of effective teamwork and to the results of the Building Blocks Questionnaire.

Part V is a source of further ideas. It tells the user where to go for further help and advice about teambuilding and will be particularly useful to those who wish to study and practise teambuilding at a deeper level than that for which the manual itself provides.

THE COMPANION VOLUME

For those who wish to organize teambuilding events I have prepared a companion volume *50 Activities for Teambuilding*. This volume, which is in looseleaf format to facilitate easy copying, contains a whole range of experiential activities which can be used to facilitate teambuilding. The activities are based on the 'Building Blocks of Effective Teamwork' outlined in Part III of this manual.

THE LANGUAGE

It is said that a psychologist is someone who tells you something you already know in a language which you cannot understand. Inevitably in any trade or profession words are used which convey a great deal to those who regularly use them but are seen as 'jargon' or 'unnecessarily technical' by those who do not. This book aims to bridge the gap between the professional who works in the team development area and the manager, team leader and team member by presenting theory and practice in a down-to-earth way.

Many managers do not read books about management because they find them dull, uninteresting and full of jargon. They also find that often they are strong on theory but weak on practice. Therefore, when I wrote the first edition of this book I established three groundrules to guide me. They were:

1 that its language should be down-to-earth, free from jargon and readily understood by those who will use it;
2 that it should strive to simplify theory;
3 that the emphasis should be on practical things which the reader can carry out within his or her own team and which he or she will find enjoyable, stimulating and useful.

I have again tried to keep to these groundrules. I hope that I have been successful and that this book will be even more useful in its revised form.

MIKE WOODCOCK

Acknowledgements

The ideas in this manual come from so many sources that it would be impossible to acknowledge them all even if I knew them, which I do not. However, where sources have been identified they have been acknowledged in the text, and references which I have found particularly valuable have been listed in Part V.

There are three special acknowledgements I wish to make. Firstly to the members of the many working teams with whom I have worked and whom I have used to test out my ideas and to study how working teams function and develop. I think particularly of the teams which I have led in my own businesses, those with which I have worked as a management development consultant and those in which I have participated or which I have visited in my Parliamentary career.

They have differed greatly and have included:

- teams offering professional services;
- teams of building trade operatives carrying out building and renovation work;
- management teams in organizations in many countries across the world with whom I have worked as a consultant;
- teams from the armed forces whom I have met on many visits to service bases in the UK, in Scandinavia and the Middle East;
- teams from the oil industry, on land and on oil production platforms in the North Sea and teams from the tobacco industry in the UK, Middle East and Africa all of whom I have studied under the auspices of the Parliament and Industry Trust;

- teams of magistrates with whom I have adjudicated in sixteen years on the magisterial bench;
- teams from the coal industry with whom I have worked as Parliamentary adviser to their trade associations;
- teams operating in the non-commercial organizations I have assisted in my work as a Member of Parliament, including charities, voluntary fund raising organizations, pressure groups, hospitals and schools;
- The House of Commons Select Committee on Trade and Industry and the many Parliamentary back bench committees and Standing Committees in which I have participated;
- teams of political activists campaigning for causes or trying to win elections;
- and many, many more teams.

All have their unique characteristics but they are all groups of people sharing common objectives and the ideas in this manual are relevant to all of them. The performance of all teams can be studied and improved.

Those I have mentioned have all contributed greatly to whatever knowledge I have on this subject.

Secondly, to Dave Francis, my partner, friend and co-author with me of a number of books about management. I am indebted to him for the many ideas which we have developed together and for his advice on the content of this book.

Finally I thank all those who have mapped out this field before me; the many writers, consultants and teachers who have continually developed ways of helping teams become more effective and on whose experience I have drawn in my work and in the preparation of this manual.

MIKE WOODCOCK

PART I
BASIC THEORY

Part I contains eight sections:

1 *What is a team?* We start with a definition of a team and consider the various types of teams commonly found in organizations.

2 *What is teamwork?* Some of the symptoms of poor teamwork are described and the characteristics of effective teamwork are outlined.

3 *The stages of team development.* The four essential stages are described to help teams to understand team development.

4 *The limitations of teambuilding.* This is included to warn that teambuilding solutions may be applied inappropriately.

5 *The role of the team leader.* The unique but essential role of the team leader is explained, priorities for effective team functioning are given and the characteristics of effective teambuilding are stated.

6 *Action planning.* A simple form of planning to help you take teambuilding decisions in a logical and sensible order.

7 *Groundrules for team development.* Some basic 'do's and don'ts' about teambuilding presented as a checklist which you can use to guide all of your teambuilding efforts.

8 *Designing teambuilding events.* To help you in planning tailor-made teambuilding events, some guidelines for designing events are included together with the principles of adult learning and their implications for teambuilding. Examples of how the theory and activities in this book can be used to form the basis of learning events are also given.

By using these eight sections you will avoid one of the serious problems of development – the potential gap between theory and practice.

1 What is a team?

Over the years that I have been working as a management consultant and writing about management topics many 'management' fashions have come and gone. Some have had little effect on the thinking of managers but others have left their mark. In 1979 when I wrote *Team Development Manual* little had been written about the subject but since then more and more has been written and more and more managers have become alive to the possibilities of improved performance through effective Teamwork. Team development is now fashionable!

The reasons are not difficult to see. As the world becomes more and more one economy so international competition becomes more severe. Opportunities are greater and so are threats. Business problems become more complex and it becomes increasingly necessary for people to work together to solve those problems. Organizations become larger as economies of scale dictate that only the biggest can take on the international competition. As they become larger so they become more complex and the necessity for people to work effectively together, often across national boundaries, becomes greater. It is those organizations which can harness the abilities of people that survive and succeed. Teamwork is the vehicle for making that happen.

A team is 'A group of people who share common objectives and who need to work together to achieve them'. Teams can be found on the sports field, in non-profit making social organizations or in commerce and industry. The primary focus of this book is team development in the working environment but the concepts and ideas can be applied wherever a group of people share common objectives and need to 'work' together in order to achieve them. They do not need to be paid to work together.

A team is not a social gathering where people meet for the purpose of enjoyment, neither is it an 'audience' of people who are assembled to listen or to learn. The House of Commons is not a team as its members do not share common objectives. Committees are not usually teams because they comprise people who represent different interest groups. Often they share concerns but they lack a unified commitment to action.

Teams can provide unique opportunities, they can make things happen which would not happen if the team did not exist.

- Like a family, they can provide support and help to their members.
- They can co-ordinate the activities of individuals.
- They can generate commitment.
- They can provide a 'place to be' so meeting a basic human need to belong.
- They can identify training and development needs.
- They can provide learning opportunities.
- They can enhance communication.
- They can provide a satisfying, stimulating and enjoyable working environment.

There can be many types of team in an organization.

Top teams

They set key objectives and develop the strategy of the organization. Because they have a broad task, they need a broad membership representing all aspects of the organization. Sometimes they may have temporary members who join them to contribute a particular expertise at a particular time.

Management teams

They set more detailed objectives and co-ordinate and control the work of others. They provide the day-to-day leadership in organizations. They need to be able to relate to the main body of members of the organization. They allocate resources and plan operations, devise development strategies and manage the boundaries between different functions.

Operator teams

These are the people who get the job done. They may work on machines or assembly lines. They may deliver goods or services. They may serve people in shops, in restaurants or on aeroplanes. They are the people who perform the primary task of the organization. They transfer inputs into outputs.

Technical teams

These are the people who set the standards in the organization. They may be technical standards, production standards or service standards but they ensure that there is a uniform approach. As organizations become larger the need for standardization becomes more apparent.

Support teams

These teams generally exist outside of the normal work flow of the organization. They provide the indirect support which is needed to enable those who 'get the job done' to operate efficiently. Often they enable control to take place.

A FURTHER WORD ABOUT TOP TEAMS

We all know that water flows downhill. Almost all organization development efforts are best started at the top. Not only will ideas flow more freely downwards than upwards but people are more likely to take the possibilities of change more seriously if they can see that those at the top are committed to it.

For many reasons trainers are reluctant to start at the top, often because access may be difficult, because trainers do not occupy a sufficiently central or senior role, because time pressures tend to be more severe at the top or simply that the trainer does not feel qualified to address top management issues. However, it is often the case that top teams are ignorant of the possibilities of team development and they are often grateful for team building interventions. Top teams are an area where many organizations choose to use external consultants who are free of day to day internal politics.

The main roles of the top team are to:

Develop strategy

- To analyse the environment and decide on the direction of the organization.
- To assess the competition and to identify business opportunities.
- To 'envision' what the future will look like, and
- To paint a picture of the possible.

Clarify values

- To decide what the organization stands for, what is right and what is wrong, and
- To keep the conscience of the organization and determine its primary motivations.

Oversee operations

- To authorize major decisions.
- To issue instructions and to monitor progress on them.
- To allocate resources and to resolve conflicts between different functions.
- To design the organization and to select its key staff, and
- To determine the remuneration and incentive packages.

Manage boundaries

To maintain high level contacts with people or organizations in the outside world.

To negotiate key agreements and to ensure that the organization has a proper place in the world, and

To seek to influence Government and/or industry policy.

All organizations need top teams. It is no accident that most large commercial organizations are run by boards of directors. People at the top level are perhaps more in need of comradeship and support than at any other level. Collective decisions need to be taken, complex problems requiring many inputs need to be addressed and the strengths and weaknesses of the organization need to be constantly addressed. The top team is the place where this can happen and unless the organization is very small it is the only place where it can happen. The ability of members of the top team to work together effectively is crucial to success. It is here that team development has the greatest potential pay-off.

2 What is teamwork?

Although it is possible to 'go it alone', the extent of human achievement is of necessity limited when people do not work together. One person can have brilliant ideas but may lack the brainpower, imagination or objectivity to capitalize on those ideas.

Organizations are essentially about people working together and yet so often they fail to capitalize upon the full potential of this. A team can accomplish much more than the sum of its individual members and yet frequently groups of people are seen to achieve less than could have been accomplished by the individual members working alone. Most organizations have meetings which dampen inspiration and departments which seem to devote more energy to maintaining their own organizational position than to the common good of the organization as a whole. Teamwork is individuals working together to accomplish more than they could alone, but, more than that, it can be exciting, satisfying and enjoyable. Perhaps the simplest analogy is with the football team. Were any of us to be given the task of building up a new national team we know that the task would involve much more than just obtaining the eleven best players in the nation. The success of the team would depend not only upon individual skills but on the way those individuals supported and worked with each other. The good football team is much more than a collection of individual skills; it is these skills used in a way which produces a united effort. Similarly, with almost any kind of team, its success, its very existence, depends upon the way in which all play together.

In recent years we have seen many approaches aimed at increasing organizational effectiveness and organizations today pay more and more attention to the training and development of their people, particularly those who hold managerial positions. Most of that development activity is centred upon the improvement of individual skills, knowledge and experience, but organizations are increasingly finding that this is not enough, that a real key to success is the way in which individuals behave towards each other and the way in which groups of people relate to and work with each other. Teamwork improves these things.

How then do we recognize where good teamwork and bad teamwork flourish? Perhaps, as with most things, it is easier to start with the bad than the good, so let us look at some of the symptoms of bad teamwork.

First, the team can have the wrong balance in its membership; essential skills are lacking, tasks are continually not accomplished efficiently. Then there is the symptom of frustration. As organizations get larger the opportunities for personal expression and satisfaction often become less. Too frequently people who work in organizations become frustrated because they can no longer see a clear way of meeting their own needs and aspirations. People just lose inspiration and lack the commitment and motivation which are essential ingredients of effective teamwork.

In many organizations the symptoms of grumbling and retaliation are easily seen. Because people cannot express themselves through the system they do it privately in discussions in the corridors, lavatories and car parks. Often bar room chat is a better indicator of organizational health than the most elaborate attitude surveys. The organizations that experience poor teamwork also seem to spend a lot of time on recriminations. They do not use mistakes as opportunities for increased learning and improvement but as excuses for punishing those who made the mistakes, and they do this in the many and varied ways in which organizations are able to hand out punishments.

Unhealthy competition is another indicator of poor teamwork. Competition is the life-blood of many organizations but there is a great difference between the kind of healthy competition where people can enjoy the just rewards of their deserved success and others can accept that the best person, system or policy succeeded, and the kind of organization where backbiting, 'dirty triks' and political infighting are the everyday pastimes of managers. Similarly great differences in rivalry between departments may be found. Many organizations owe much of their success to the natural competitive spirit which exists between departments and to the pride of team membership which departmentalization often brings, but many others have departments which are at constant war with each other, each jockeying for superior organizational position, influence or perks. One particular organization was characterized for many years by the constant bickering and 'dirty tricks' of its heads of departments, each departmental head taking advantage over the others whenever possible. Not only did that lead to the organization as a whole missing opportunities, but many more junior employees found that although they wanted to work with others organizational barriers had been erected between them and their counterparts in other departments.

Another sound indicator of poor teamwork is simply the expression which employees wear on their faces. Effective teamwork breeds happiness and the uniformed visitor can often get an immediate impression of whether work is a happy place to be or whether being 'killed in the rush' at 'clocking off' time is a risk. Work does not have to be a dull and unenjoyable place; it can so easily be a really rewarding place where people love to be.

To many who have studied organizations, openness and honesty are the key indicators of organizational health. Unfortunately, some people seem to try honesty only when everything else has failed. Many managers particularly seem to go to enormous lengths to avoid telling the truth. There are, of course, occasions in every organization where something other than total openness is necessary but where good teamwork exists there is generally no need for locks on drawers, dishonest statements to employees and the taking of false bargaining stances.

Meetings are another key indicator of teamwork. The main reason for having meetings is to utilize the collective skills of a group of people whilst working on common problems or opportunities. Too often, however, we experience meetings which in no way use these skills, meetings where only one or a few people contribute, and meetings where many managers seem to use the occasion as an opportunity to lay down the rules rather than utilize the resources of the team. The quality of meetings can usually be determined by the way in which individuals either look foward to or dread the normal weekly or monthly get together.

In many organizations the quality of relationship between managers and those they manage is so low that effective teamwork just cannot get off the ground. Where people cannot confide in or trust their manager, where they are fearful or where their conversations are on a superficial or trivial level then real teamwork is unlikely to exist. Good teamwork engenders high quality relationships. Another sign of low quality relationships is often that the leader becomes increasingly isolated from the team, failing to represent their view while they do not subscribe to his or hers. The effective team leader needs to be very much a part of the team,

People just not developing is another sure sign of ineffective teamwork. If a team is to be effective it needs to be continually developing itself and this in part means constantly facilitating individual as well as team development. Often development does not happen because:

(a)   there are perceived or real time pressures;
(b)   it is seen as the job of the personnel department or training officer;
(c)   conflict exists between the team's culture and that of the organisation;
(d)   team leaders lack the skills or willingness to make it happen;
(e)   there is fear of the consequences of development.

Sometimes poor teamwork results in jobs getting done twice or not at all because no clear understanding of roles within and between teams exists. Sometimes although common problems exist people are just not able or willing to get together and work on them.

Then there is the attitude which teams and individual members have to the possibility of external help. The ineffective team will usually either reject offers of help because it fears the consequences of outsiders finding out what the team is really like or will seize all offers of help because it lacks any coherent view of how to proceed and is content to hand over its problems to someone else. The effective team will use external help constructively by recognizing the unique contribution and viewpoint which it can bring, but it will always maintain ownership of its own problems and its own destiny.

Creativity is a delicate flower which only flourishes in the right conditions, mainly conditions of personal freedom and support; freedom to experiment, try out ideas and concepts and support from those who listen, evaluate and offer help. A dearth of new ideas generally goes with poor teamwork because it is within teams that the conditions for creativity can most easily be created.

The degree to which people help and use each other is another indicator. Where effective teamwork does not exist people tend to work in isolation and neither offer nor receive the help of their colleagues. All of us need that help in order to perform at our optimum level.

The conditions described above are indicative of an unhealthy organization and all of them can be significantly improved by effective teamwork.

What then are the characteristics of effective teamwork? Very simply they are the opposites of what is described above.

The team has the right balance of skills, ability and aspirations. People can and do express themselves honestly and openly. Conversation about work is the same both inside and outside the organization. Mistakes are faced openly and used as vehicles for learning and difficult situations are confronted.

Helpful competition and conflict of ideas are used constructively and team members have a pride in the success of their team. Unhelpful competition and conflict have been eliminated.

Good relationships exist with other teams and departments. Each values and respects the other and their respective leaders themselves comprise an effective team.

Personal relationships are characterized by support and trust, with people helping each other whenever possible.

Meetings are productive and stimulating with all participating and feeling ownership of the actions which result from the decisions made. New ideas abound and their use enables the team to stay ahead.

Boss–subordinate relationships are sound, each helping the other to perform each role better, and the team feels that it is led in an appropriate way.

Personal and individual development is highly rated and opportunities are constantly sought for making development happen.

There is clear agreement about and understanding of objectives and of the roles which the team and its individual members will play in achieving them.

External help will be welcomed and used where appropriate.

Finally, the team regularly reviews where it is going, why it needs to go there, and how it is getting there. If necessary, it alters its practices in the light of that review. Finally, communication is effected up, down and across the organization and with the outside world.

All of this means that 'work' is a happy place to be; people enjoy themselves wherever possible but this enjoyment is conducive to achievement, not a barrier to it. People get satisfaction from their working lives and work is one of the places where they meet their needs and aspirations.

These characteristics can be seen as the raw materials of effective teamwork. I like to see them as 'building blocks' because they are what we can use in a very practical way to build effective teams. Stated as simply as possible they are –

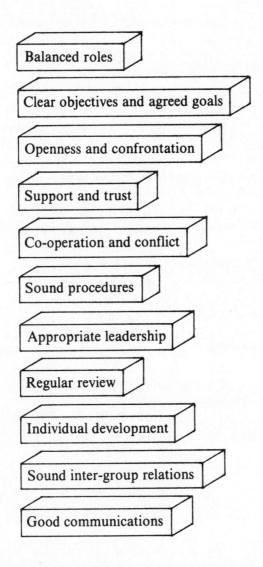

In Part III of this manual there is a detailed commentary on each of these building blocks.

WHEN TO USE A TEAM APPROACH

Almost all organizational tasks demand teamwork but it is possible to identify those situations where a team approach is particularly productive:

> *When people work in relative isolation.* Salespeople usually operate in relative isolation and have a need to feel that they belong to a team.
> *When the job is complex.* Requiring a combination of skills and effort from a range of individuals.
> *When decision making needs to be collective.* Often effective decision making requires inputs from many sources.
> *When consensus is important.* It can be argued that consensus is always important. Japanese success in commercial ventures is often ascribed to the commitment to consensus. Many Japanese organizations will spend considerable time and effort in achieving consensus before moving forward with any new development. Success is easier to achieve when all are on one side.
> *When hierarchical relationships are less potent.* Teams are a better vehicle for increasing motivation and enabling complex reporting relationships to develop.
> *When problems are broad.* Requiring a broad range of expertise. Most large companies have boards of directors – top teams.
> *When support is needed.* When morale depends on support from others or where people are unable to operate alone, teams can provide the vehicle for meeting needs.
> *When individual strengths and weaknesses are difficult to identify.* Teams can facilitate a better understanding of how to alleviate weaknesses and develop strengths.
> *When important development needs occur.* Teams are efficient vehicles for meeting 'shared' training needs.

3 The stages of team development

As teams become increasingly effective so the characteristics they display and the procedures they adopt also change. Even where teams have not tried consciously to improve their methods of operation and effectiveness there can be tremendous differences, but where serious efforts are made to improve these things observers have noted that there are common characteristics which tend to be exhibited according to the stage of development. Before exhibiting the signs of effective teamwork which were listed in '1 What is teamwork?' often a team will need to pass through several stages of development during which other signs or characteristics will be exhibited.

Any attempt at defining these stages and the characteristics associated with them must be an over-simplification. However, a simple model based on four essential stages of development is very useful in helping teams to understand team development and also to understand and agree where they are in the development process. It must be remembered, however, that no team ever exhibits solely the characteristics of one particular stage, rather it is a question of which characteristics are the most prominent. A grouping, even though crude, does help a team to understand something of where it is in the development process and of where it wants to be, and many have found this simple four-stage model useful (see page 21).

STAGE 1: THE UNDEVELOPED TEAM

This is the most common stage of development to be found in

organizations. It abounds wherever people have come together to complete a task but have devoted little or no time to considering how they should or do operate.

One characteristic of this stage is that feelings are not dealt with, usually because it is not seen as appropriate to consider the way others feel and certainly not to discuss feelings openly. Generally, emotions are seen as something only appropriate to one's private life with the workplace being for work. If feelings and emotions do come to the fore they are usually immediately brushed under the carpet. People conform to the established line, often because that is the way in which things have always been done and sometimes because they are too scared to suggest changes. Even constructive ideas about change are not welcomed and people usually learn that it is safer not to 'rock the boat' by making unwanted suggestions. This usually results in people being disheartened and leadership seldom being challenged. Little care is shown for other people or their views and this is frequently characterized by a lot of talking and little real listening. Meetings tend to comprise a series of statements with people queuing to put their point of view without listening to what goes before or after. Personal weaknesses are covered up because the group lacks the skill to support or to eliminate them. Mistakes are used as 'evidence' to help convict people rather than as opportunities to learn. There is no shared understanding of what needs to be done and often the leader has a different view from those being led. Where there is clarity this is often because people's instructions have come from the top rather than because they have shared in the determination of plans. Mistakes are frequently covered up by individuals as they know that they will be seen as failure and this means that team members do not get the opportunity to learn from their mistakes and improve. Outside threats are met by defensiveness, increased bureaucracy, paperwork and rules. People confine themselves to their own defined jobs and the boss takes most of the decisions.

It needs to be said that many apparently effective teams show these characteristics, but this is usual only if the boss has the wisdom, energy and time to make all the decisions. This is not real teamwork as it does not capitalize on the dormant strengths of the team. Sometimes this stage is referred to as the 'king and court' stage because the team resembles the old concept of the 'court' who would never dare to challenge the judgement of their 'king'.

The greatest single leap forward in team development is when a team leaves stage 1 and enters stage 2 because that is when it takes a decision to do something serious about improving things.

STAGE 2: THE EXPERIMENTING TEAM

Stage 2 can begin when the team decides that it wants seriously to review its operating methods and undertake activities which will improve its performance. It is this willingness which is the distinguishing characteristic of the stage 2 team. The team begins to be willing to experiment; to sail in what, for them, are uncharted waters, and face the ensuing opportunities and dangers. Other features of this stage of development are that problems are faced more openly and wider options are considered before decisions are taken. Where necessary the underlying values and beliefs affecting decisions begin to be debated and this often leads to temporary feelings of insecurity and high risks. As more risky issues are opened up hitherto taboo topics begin to be discussed and often the way in which the team is managed is one of the first issues examined. More personal issues are raised, feelings begin to be considered and personal animosities begin to be dealt with. People begin to say things which they may have wanted to mention for years. This can obviously lead to some traumatic encounters between team members but they quickly learn that when the dirt has been put on the table and examined the team becomes a healthier and happier place to be.

The group inevitably becomes more inward looking, and for a time may even reject other groups and individuals. This is a transient phase and is because the team has become so interested and obsessed with its own problems and new horizons that it just wants to work on them and sees that as the most important thing to do. More concern is shown for the views and problems of colleagues with a consequent increase in real listening, and, often for the first time, people begin to understand other members of the team. Meetings begin to be characterized by more listening and thinking and less talking. In this stage teams can often become uncomfortable but they are also dynamic and exciting. The observer can see things coming to life and people who have been dormant for years start to contribute. However, although the team has become more open and potentially more effective it still lacks the capacity to act in an economic, unified and methodical way.

It has worked on some of the interpersonal issues successfully but it has not yet put this learning to profitable use.

STAGE 3: THE CONSOLIDATING TEAM

After the team has worked on the interpersonal issues of stage 2 and has begun to resolve them it will begin to have the confidence, open approach and trust to examine its operating methods. Generally the team decides to adopt a more systematic approach which leads to a clearer and more methodical way of working. The rules and procedures which characterized stage 1 now begin to be re-introduced but this time they are not edicts from on high or historical precedents which have to be observed, they are the agreed operating rules of the team, which everyone has had a part in framing and to which everyone is committed. Even with the better relationships built in stage 2, the team quickly learns that groundrules are still important. The most apparent evidence of this is the way in which decisions are taken, usually by:

(a) clarifying the purpose of the task or activity;
(b) establishing the objectives which need to be met;
(c) collecting the information which will be needed;
(d) considering the options which are open to the team;
(e) detailed planning of what needs to be done;
(f) reviewing the outcome and using it as a basis for improving future operations.

The improved relationships and more exciting methods experienced in stage 2 are maintained but they are used to build the groundrules and working procedures which the team will use.

STAGE 4: THE MATURE TEAM

After stage 3 has been worked through there is the basis for a really mature team. The openness, concern and improved relationships of stage 2 and the systematic approach of stage 3 can now be used to complete the task of building a really mature team.

Flexibility becomes the keynote, with different procedures being adopted to meet different needs. People are not concerned with defending positions. Leadership is decided by the situation not protocol, the group itself recognizing the kind of leadership which is necessary and the leader recognizing the need to involve the team in matters of substance. Often formal management hierarchy is abandoned in favour of something which the team feels is more appropriate. Everyone's energies are utilized for the team, because individual commitment to team success exists. There is pride in the team and its achievements but this does not stifle individual initiative and achievement because everyone realizes that people are happier and more effective when they are able to meet their needs and aspirations. The team considers essential principles and social aspects of its decisions. It realizes not only that it is part of a larger organization but also that organizations have a moral and social responsibility. It begins to realize that it is part of a big world and can can help others as well. Development becomes an increasing priority because all realize that continued success depends on continued development. Trust, openness, honesty, co-operation and confront-ation, and a continual review of results become part of the way of life. The desire to improve further means that external help is always welcome. The team is not only admired but is emulated and it is always willing to reach out and help other less mature teams. Above all the team is a happy and rewarding place to be.

HELPING TEAMS THROUGH THE STAGES OF TEAM DEVELOPMENT

Team leaders and trainers need to help their teams to move through the various stages of team development and whilst the path may not be entirely predictable there are actions which can be taken to enhance progress at each stage.

Stage 1 The undeveloped team

- Facilitate 'getting to know you' exercises, stimulating greater personal knowledge.
- Demonstrate openness by example.
- Invite members to share their concerns and problems.
- Encourage consideration of individual strengths and weaknesses.
- Make team activities enjoyable.
- Give maximum support.

Stage 2 The experimenting team

- Encourage greater openness.

- Begin to involve team members in review of team performance.
- Build bridges between individuals.
- Allow conflicts to surface.
- Question decision making and problem solving methods.
- Find opportunities to experiment.
- Give high level of support.
- Encourage individual team members to 'air their grievances'.
- Seek common ground.

Stage 3 The consolidating team

- Develop problem solving skills.
- Develop decision making strategies.
- Develop individual skills.
- Develop a capacity for the team to compensate for individual weaknesses.
- Encourage people to share strengths.
- Celebrate successes.
- Clarify objectives.
- Regularly review performance and plan improvements in team functioning.
- Give moderate support.

Stage 4 The mature team

- Build bridges with other teams.
- Experiment with different forms of leadership.
- Allow leadership to change with the needs of the task.
- Clarify values.
- Consider the possibilities of enhanced inputs into the organization.
- Encourage informal communications.
- Fight insularity.
- Expose team functioning to external scrutiny.
- Give minimal support.

The team development clock

The process of team development can be seen as a clock face with the undeveloped team starting at midnight and complete maturity being achieved within 24 hours. A useful way to relate the theory to your

Stage 4	Experimentation. Risky issues debated. Wider options considered. Personal feelings raised. More listening. Concern for others.	plus	Methodical working. Agreed procedures Established groundrules.	plus	High flexibility. Appropriate leadership. Maximum use of energy and ability. Essential principles and social aspects considered. Needs of all met. Development a priority.
Stage 3	Experimentation. Risky issues debated. Wider options considered. Personal feelings raised. More listening. Concern for others.	plus	Methodical working. Agreed procedures. Established groundrules.		
Stage 2	Experimentation. Risky issues debated. Wider options considered. Personal feelings raised. More listening. Concern for others.				
Stage 1	Feelings not dealt with. Workplace is for work. Established line prevails. No 'rocking the boat'. Poor listening. Weaknesses covered up. Unclear objectives. Low involvement in planning. Bureaucracy. Boss takes most decisions.				

Summary of the four stages of team development

own situation is by considering the position on the clock face of a team or teams of which you are a member. Whatever stage of team development you are in, try to assess the degree to which you have worked through it on the path to the next stage.

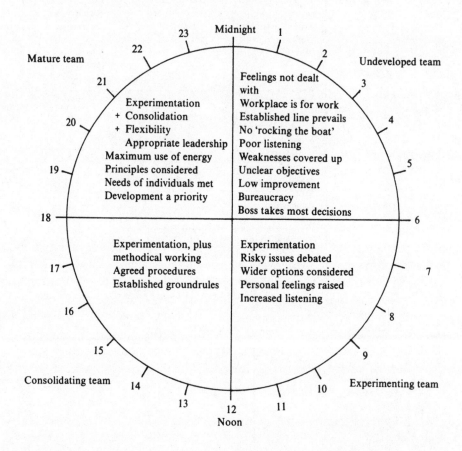

Next relate the stage of development of the team(s) to the list of actions on the previous pages, identifying those which are and are not being utilized.

4   The limitations of teambuilding

Reading only a few current management magazines is sufficient to indicate which of the various techniques or theories for improving the effectiveness of individuals or organizations are in fashion. It is perhaps inevitable that writers, advisers and people whose profession is helping organizations themselves become relatively easily interested in new or exciting theories and techniques. Unfortunately, the victims of their enthusiasm are often those whom they seek to help. Many advisers and consultants are known to tour the country with a solution in their briefcase looking for a problem to fit it, and often they find such a problem whether or not it really exists. Similarly, in some organizations there are training officers who are tempted to see problems which are not there simply to try out a new technique which particularly appeals to them.

Teamwork is increasingly being seen as an important subject and teambuilding is now one of the most popular and effective ways of improving the health of an organization. There is then a very acute danger that teambuilding solutions may be applied inappropriately, that well-meaning but misdirected people may go through the 'ritual dances' of teambuilding when the problems of the organization are really quite different.

I have led a great many 'teambuilding workshops', events at which managers, directors and training officers have been introduced to the theory of teambuilding. All have been characterized by the enthusiasm which is generated and the desire of participants to engage in teambuilding activities not only at the event but also when they returned to their organizations. Because of this I have always insisted on including a session which aims to put teamwork problems into the context of the whole range of 'people problems' which an organization may face. It is so easy to rush into teambuilding activities when teamwork is not the problem.

There are many definitions and models of the 'people problems' which organizations can face but the one which I generally use was developed by Dave Francis and myself and is explained in greater detail in *Unblocking your Organisation.*

The aim of this chapter is not to explore other problems but merely to show that there are many issues to do with people which organizations commonly face and which will not be solved solely by improved teamwork. It is true that, to a certain extent, all 'people problems' are interrelated and any solutions will overlap but it is also important that before taking action there is agreement that teamwork is central to the problem. Although improved teamwork will help people to confront and solve almost any problem the following ten groups of 'people problems' will not be solved solely by the kind of approaches contained in this book, because they are not essentially teamwork problems.

POOR RECRUITMENT AND SELECTION

Whenever a business operates people have to be hired and, although most organizations have vast experience of this area, so often the root of an organization's 'people problems' lies simply in the wrong people being selected. Either they have the wrong skills or the wrong personality. Sometimes those who carry out the selection lack the required skills, sometimes they are the wrong people to be making the selection, and sometimes the organization is unclear about the kind of people it really requires. Often, in spite of elaborate personnel departments, policies and procedures are unclear. No amount of teambuilding will make square pegs fit round holes!

CONFUSED ORGANIZATION STRUCTURE

Everything bigger than a one man unit needs some organization. It can take many forms but most businesses tend to be based on a hierarchical system. Usually the boss sits at the top and other levels of management span out like a pyramid. Usually lines of responsibility and authority are clearly and explicitly stated. Hierarchical organizations are usually fine where repetitive tasks need to be accomplished and deadlines need to be met but can be disastrous where creativity and initiative are required and where innovation is the keynote of success. Here a more flexible, free-ranging organizational form is often required which will enable people to experiment, to step out of line and fly their own kites. If the way people are organized is alien to the task being performed, again teambuilding will do little more than expose the problem; it will not in itself solve it.

One particular organization continually faced a dilemma in the way in which it was organized. Fundamentally, this organization needed to have new ideas, to develop them and to experiment and then to apply them. Although the greater part of the organization was, and always would be, engaged in applying the developed ideas, it needed as its very lifeblood the creative people who could conceive new approaches and experiment with and develop them. Here was the classic example of a group of highly creative people who required freedom to experiment, living alongside a group of people who needed to produce results and meet deadlines. For years the whole organization constantly moved between an organizational form which was conducive to the work of the first group and one which suited the second. When creativity was suited complaints of sloppiness, passed deadlines and low output came to the fore. This resulted in a tighter, more controllable structure which in turn stifled the creative people and led to fewer ideas, less experimentation and less development. Managers regularly nailed their colours to one mast or the other and careers were made and lost with increasing rapidity as the pendulum kept swinging. Eventually the organization came to its senses and recognized that both approaches were right and that it had to live with two different organizational forms. The ideas and development people opted for a 'matrix' organization, in this case one in which each person had two lines of responsibility, one to a line manager and one to a development leader. The others opted for a more conventional 'hierarchical' organizational form. One basis for effective teamwork was thus formed.

Another symptom of poor organization is the 'over-developed limb'. Sometimes a particular department, function or individual becomes so powerful that their part of the organization becomes far too large or influential for the good of the whole. It is like a body with an arm which is twice as long as it should be – the whole is handicapped by the part. Problems like this need to be dealt with before effective teamwork across an organization can begin.

LACK OF CONTROL

This is often very similar to, and related to, poor organization because it is through organization that control is usually exercised. The way in which people are 'controlled' can be either a very positive or a very negative force. Over-control can lead to initiative being stifled and potentially valuable contributions being lost. Most people are quite capable of controlling their own contributions and actions within a reasonably loose framework of overall accountability and, naturally, they resent unnecessary external controls. However, most people also recognize the necessity for sensible control and do not resent control which is in the right hands and which is understood and agreed. They realize that an organization which is out of control is like a ship in a storm without a rudder. Teambuilding in an atmosphere of over-control will not work because people will lack the basic freedom either to agree principles or to put them into practice. Similarly, it will not work in an atmosphere of anarchy where no basic disciplines are accepted or used.

POOR TRAINING

Keeping up with present-day changes is an ever-increasing problem for today's managers, often requiring more and more learning to be undertaken in little available time. One of the hallmarks of an effective team is that the skills and knowledge of its participants are continually reviewed, updated and improved, but everyone needs certain skills and some knowledge to even begin playing their part in a team. In most organizations there are induction courses and facilities for initial training, coupled with facilities for ensuring that people are able to attend external events and so obtain the skills and knowledge which the organization cannot impart. Effective teambuilding can help identify both deficiencies and opportunities for increased learning and also help personal development, but it will not take the place of the fundamental learning opportunities which every organization needs to give to its employees. Crucial to teambuilding is the learning climate and the overall receptivity to learning. Before almost any development activity can take place people need to welcome new learning and not feel threatened by it. Before team development can take place, training policy methods and practice need to be resolved.

LOW MOTIVATION

The way people feel about the organization they work in has a great deal to do with the amount of effort they are prepared to put into their working lives. Employees' views about the organization they work for are often formed even before they enter through the door. For example, the organization may have a reputation in the local or the national community, and it will have its own recruitment practices. The moment a new employee walks through the door he or she really starts to form, alter or confirm an opinion, based on the experiences met. An immediate impression may be gained of the level of motivation in many organizations. In some places you could be 'killed in the rush' as people depart when the 5 p.m. bell rings. To them work is a chore and they are willing to expend only the minimum necessary effort in accomplishing it. To achieve high motivation there needs to be a rough match between personal and organizational aims and it is this match that many 'motivation' schemes seek to achieve. For years managers have debated what brings about high motivation, with some managers still believing that clean toilets and works outings are the key to success whilst others believe that participation in decision making or co-ownership are the answers. But all agree that motivation is very, very important and without it any organization undertaking teambuilding would be wasting its time and resources because people would not be prepared to put in the necessary time and effort.

LOW CREATIVITY

How creative people are depends on a whole range of things, not least of all high motivation and freedom from bureaucratic controls. Teambuilding can play an important part in originating the kind of climate in which creativity can flourish, but it is not solely a question of teamwork. In particular, people need to know that ideas will be welcomed and valued. The signs of low creativity are easily recognizable, for example, empty suggestion boxes, dull meetings, lack of new products, yesterday's practices, and competitors having all the new development ideas. Lack of creativity can partly be caused by poor teamwork but it can also have at its root wrong people, restrictive management or simply too much concern for the present and too little for the future.

INAPPROPRIATE MANAGEMENT PHILOSOPHY

Management philosophy starts at the top. If the top managers in an organization hold views about people at work which prevent management being exercised in an open, honest and supportive manner then real teamwork is unlikely to get off the ground. We may take, as an example, a particular teambuilding assignment in a factory where the MD presented the problem of managers not working effectively together. The MD saw bickering and hostility in the workforce but the workers had a very different view. Individually, they said that the MD worked on the 'divide and rule' principle, believing that managers needed constant threats to motivate them; by such actions any chances of teamwork were destroyed. In short, they felt that these beliefs about people and the way these were acted out were alien to the principles of effective teamwork. Happily, a few months later, the seeds of real teamwork were beginning to germinate in that organization but the main factor which brought that about was a change in the basic assumptions and beliefs of that MD. The project turned out to be one which was really about helping one individual to manage people in a different way, motivating rather than demotivating.

LACK OF SUCCESSION PLANNING AND DEVELOPMENT

These problems are really a step further on from those of recruitment and selection. People need to grow with the firm and systematically take on bigger responsibilities. If they do not, then inevitably there will be a shortage of people of the right calibre to staff key positions. Effective teamwork is important throughout an organization but it is critical at management level and without management succession and development the organization will be without the raw material for a really effective top management team.

UNCLEAR AIMS

Teams exist to undertake tasks, and without a task no team has a basis for existence. It necessarily follows that any organization wishing to build effective teams needs a clear view of where it wants to go and why. Highly developed teams without an aim will quickly degenerate and groups of people without a task will never be able to practise true teamwork.

UNFAIR REWARDS

In an organization the way people are valued is largely shown by the rewards given to them, and unless people are of independent means then pay is by far the most important part of the reward package. However, there are other more subtle rewards which an organization can confer on its staff. Holidays, cars, offices, even secretaries are seen by many as very important rewards. There are also many subtle punishments which organizations can hand out to those whose contribution is not so valued. Almost everyone feels underpaid and undervalued at some time especially when they see others, whose worth to the organization they would put lower than their own, receiving a better 'reward package' than themselves. I have never yet seen a totally equitable reward system but obviously inequitable rewards should be tackled before effective teamwork can flourish. In the words of the old saying, 'if you pay peanuts you get monkeys', ... and by contrast today's organizations need to be staffed by effective teams of men and women.

PERSONAL STAGNATION

If a team is to be an effective force individual members need to be open and alive to the possibilities of personal development. People who are not developing as individuals are stagnating and stagnating people hold back the rest of the team. It is not a question of a lack of skills but of having the attitudes towards working life which are conducive to personal effectiveness and growth. Some symptoms of personal stagnation are the avoidance of personal challenge, contentment with low standards, avoidance of risk taking, misuse of time and energy, intolerance to the views of others and generally being out of touch with ones own feelings. Teams which have people who are personally stagnating need to deal with the problem before effective teambuilding can commence. Excellent performance is rarely obtained from individuals unless they have an active and open approach to their working lives.

The above list may seem formidable and managers would be correct in taking the view that if all of them needed to be right before effective teamwork could commence then the idea would be better forgotten. Effective teamwork is linked to all of them because they all concern people and the things they do in organizations. Any work on teambuilding will usually lead to organizational health but whilst it can make a significant contribution it will not solve all the 'people problems' which are commonly found in organizations.

REFERENCE

Woodcock, M. and Francis, D., *Unblocking Your Organisation*, University Associates, la Jolla, 1975.

5   The role of the team leader

As I write this section I am sitting on a beach in Cotonou in the Republic of Benin, a self-proclaimed Marxist People's Republic. The main purpose of my visit is to see how one British exporter maintains and develops its team of representatives in this, one of the least visited of West African countries. Earlier I visited Dahomey to see the remains of the palaces of the ancient kings of Dahomey who ruled in this part of the world until the turn of the century. Each of the kings who ruled over the 600 years of the dynasty was an effective team leader. He led his people in battle, met what he and his advisers perceived to be their needs and commanded universal loyalty, trust and support. Each king was expected to show his virility by taking at least 4000 wives and his harem was tended by 300 eunuchs. Each time he sought guidance from his gods he sacrificed 21 humans as a mark of respect and anyone who cast his eye on any of his wives was immediately beheaded.

When the king died, 41 of his wives were chosen for the honour of accompanying him to the 'hereafter'. Their fate was to be buried alive and yet such was the 'commitment to the team' that the wives fought for the honour of being put to death. Team leaders have existed since the dawn of civilization but the leadership styles and methods they have employed have varied considerably. Many managers would perhaps like to adopt some of the customs of the kings of Dahomey but today they are unlikely to be successful.

The leader has a unique and crucial role in the development of any team. Team members watch their leader's management styles and evaluate his or her ability to promote openness, co-operation and team debate. A manager may announce an intention to adopt team management principles but then behave in ways that clearly demonstrate a lack of trust in individuals. Without effort, personal integrity and trust, a team cannot be developed. A team leader must also be able to demonstrate some expertise in a subject important to the team. He or she will also need process skills. Any teambuilding efforts are likely to be ineffective unless the team leader is committed to the process of deciding whether to use a team development approach. The initial step should be to assess whether it is worth the cost and effort required (see Woodcock and Francis, 1981). Each team should be examined to determine whether it is receptive and significant. The following chart indicates which groups are most likely to benefit from team development.

Priority for effective functioning

As a team	Team character
Very high priority	Team members are highly interdependent and are collectively responsible for achieving major objectives that have a significant effect on the organization's profitability or effectiveness. Team members must work well together to achieve results. Survival of the organization would be prejudiced by failure.
High priority	Team members are interdependent and need to be effective and competent to perform. The team makes a significant contribution to organizational effectiveness. Poor performance would lead to wasted opportunities and low morale.
Medium priority	The team has clear objectives but can achieve success without high levels of interdependency. Team members have distinct roles with individual responsibilities and each contributes to the team as an 'expert'.

As a team	Team character
Low priority	The team exists but its performance as a team has only a minor impact on the success of the enterprise. However, team development would benefit morale and motivation.
Very low priority	The team is a loose grouping that lacks a shared objective and is relatively unimportant in the organization. Competence has little relationship to team effectiveness because individual performance is the key factor.

The team leader must be aware of the needs of the group and have sufficient understanding of the concept of team building to steer the group through a series of developmental stages. An open approach is vital. All issues affecting the group must be talked through, feedback given and received and time spent clarifying expectations. The team leader must demonstrate the high level of openness that is an essential characteristic of the team approach and be watchful toward team members, identifying their individual needs and enabling each to be developed and strengthened as the work of the team continues.

In essence the team leader's role is to ensure that the team has the right blend of roles, that skills are developed, that co-operation and support are maximized and that each individual makes his optimum contribution.

It is important to ensure that the following guidelines are followed:

- all team members are clear about the objectives of the team;
- individual skills are identified and roles clarified;
- the team is structured appropriately for the needs of the task;
- the team reflects on its work methods and sets targets for improvement;
- the team develops a self-discipline that uses time and resources well;
- the team has sufficient opportunities to meet and work through problems;
- the team supports members and develops close relationships; and
- the team has open relationships and is prepared to confront difficulties and blockages to effectiveness.

The primary role of the team leader is to motivate individual team members and not all team members will be motivated by the same needs. The lower down an organization the more difficult it is to align individual and organizational needs. For example, at senior levels the need for profit will be recognized in a commercial organization. However, at shop floor level the interests of the shareholders will be less of a reality.

Whilst all contribute towards profitability the link is easier to see and to understand at management levels. Most people in work settings are motivated by four principal needs.

1 *The need for remuneration.* Most employees go to work for money and if they perceive themselves to be undervalued in terms of the pay that they receive they are unlikely to be highly motivated. Of course, one person's acceptable goal may not be another's, social background, regional and industrial differences can make a big difference, but the old adage is generally true: 'if you pay peanuts you get monkeys'. Monetary incentives do work, but they are more effective where performance is easily measured, as with a sales force or with production operatives. Within remuneration we can include so called hygene factors and fringe benefits. By the first we mean things like working environment, canteen facilities, sickness schemes, etc. Research suggest that these are not key motivators but they can act as de-motivators where they are of an unacceptable standard. It is necessary to get them right before real motivators can be applied. By fringe benefits we mean items which are given in lieu of pay, although some may be necessary for adequate performance. Items such as private health care, retirement plans, company cars and low interest finance fit into this category. Often they are a very tax efficient way of motivating people, particularly at senior levels.

2 *The need for belonging.* Since pre-historic times men have hunted in groups and few people like to work alone. People like to feel that they have a place in an organization, to know where they belong. The work team can provide many of the advantages of family life offering affection, support, warmth, friendship and guidance. The effective team leader is rather like the head of the family ensuring that the family unit meets the needs of its individual members, that they can grow and develop and that they have a retreat from the threat of the outside world.

3 *The need for significance.* Not only do people feel a need to belong but they also have a need to feel that their contribution is significant. It does not have to be the 'best' or 'most valuable' contribution but it does need to be meaningful and this in time brings respect from other team members. Job satisfaction was a popular phrase during the 1970's and many programmes were introduced into companies in attempts to make people derive more satisfaction from the work they were doing. In essence, job satisfaction is derived from contribution which is felt to be 'significant'.

4 *The need for achievement.* We all like to win and winning in itself provides the stimulus to achieve higher standards and to win, again and again. Jones and Jongeward in their book *Born to Win* describe how individuals can be categorized as 'Winners' and 'Losers' and how people who adopt a winning stance towards life are much more likely to win than those who adopt a losing stance. In large measure it is a self-fulfilling prophecy. The same is true of teams and it is largely up to the team leader to ensure that the team adopts a 'winning stance'. 'Success breeds success' as they say, but without it individuals can miss out on one of their basic needs: the need to achieve.

These needs are present in all of us to lesser and greater degrees and it is one of the roles of the team leader to find out what 'turns on' his team members. Only then can he use the optimum motivational techniques.

Good team leaders have a personal commitment to relate with others directly and honestly. Few roles in society expose the integrity of an individual as extensively as management. Team leaders who use their power for manipulation, demoralizing others, or restricting potential are soon detected, scorned and mistrusted. Trust is crucial to the development of a healthy and productive team. Trust is built by people saying what they mean and rooting out areas of uncertainty or operational weakness. Although techniques of leadership may be taught, each individual needs to clarify and express an approach that is strictly personal and consistent with held values. Team leaders who are mature and effective have developed a deep-rooted personal approach appropriate to the task that is warm yet open, confronting and problem-solving and sets high standards for others and self.

Teambuilding skills are relevant to all organizations that need to combine individual talents to achieve common goals. Many managers and supervisors spend more than sixty per cent of their time in meetings or otherwise operating in a group. Such managers need a team approach to achieve their objectives, in particular managers of project groups, development teams, policy groups, service functions, and groups working under pressure. Teambuilding skills are particularly important when a number of individuals must be brought together and learn to work co-operatively and effectively on common tasks. This frequently involves chairing meetings, representing groups and developing good relationships with other units in the organization. A manager consciously develops a team approach by sharing problems, developing a positive climate, clarifying goals and reviewing effectiveness regularly. These skills are most used when people are highly dependent on each other and need to work well together to achieve a high standard of output.

Other managers and supervisors work in relative isolation, perhaps contributing technical expertise, and they have less need for teambuilding skills.

Teambuilding is a positive management tool because it generates a high energy group that is resourceful, effective and responsive. Team leaders who are competent to undertake team building activities tend to show the following characteristics:

- they have a high level of leadership skills,
- they are consistent,
- they support a team philosophy,
- they take great care to select appropriate members for their teams,
- they are committed to the development and welfare of team members,
- they build a positive climate,
- they are motivated by achievement,
- they clearly define team roles,
- they use effective work methods,
- they clearly define individual roles,
- they review performance without resorting to personal criticism,
- they encourage individual development,
- they encourage creative potential,
- they develop sound relationships with other teams,
- they use conflict constructively,
- they encourage controlled risk taking,

- they seek feedback,
- they use time well,
- they establish high standards.

Conversely, team leaders who display the following characteristics are poorly equipped to undertake team building:

- their leadership skills are weak,
- they are inconsistent,
- they do not really believe in a team philosophy,
- they select inappropriate members for their teams,
- they lack commitment to the development of other team members,
- they fail to build a positive climate,
- they are not motivated by high achievement,
- they do not clearly define the role of their team,
- their work methods are suspect,
- they fail to define individual roles,
- they combine criticism and review,
- they pay insufficient attention to the development of team members,
- they subdue creative potential,
- they tolerate poor relationships with other teams,
- they use conflict disruptively,
- they discourage risk taking,
- they avoid personal feedback,
- they use time badly,
- they permit low standards.

REFERENCE

Woodcock, M. and Francis, D., *Organisation Development through Teambuilding*, Gower, Aldershot, 1981.

6 Action planning

Action planning is vital if your teambuilding efforts are to succeed. It also needs to be part of a simple framework which includes identification of needs and subsequent review of action. In any development activity the simple framework shown below should always be kept in mind.

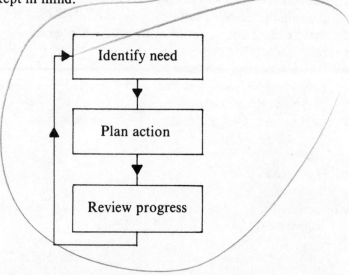

Simple action-planning framework

It is not advisable to start action planning until you have identified a need and always review progress during and after the action. Action planning can be as simple as following the checklist of questions given below, an approach which will help ensure that:

needs are identified;
needs are agreed;
the right people are involved;
action is practical and appropriate;
the right resources are used;
other implications are considered;
the right time scale is adopted;
results are used as a basis for further improvement.

CHECKLIST APPROACH TO ACTION PLANNING

Some typical examples are listed below each question.

1 *What is the need?*
To improve openness.
To develop a more effective form of leadership.
To improve our decision-making ability.
To clarify our objectives.
To generally review and improve the way we operate as a team.

2 *Is this need agreed by those affected?*
Has everyone been consulted?
Have we ensured commitment?
Do we have to spend more time agreeing needs?

3 *To whom does it apply?*
The whole team.
Leaders of different teams.
Task groups.
An individual.

4 *How will we know if we have been successful?*
Are we sure of our development objectives?
Are they measurable?
Can other people help us to evaluate?
What behavioural changes do we expect?

5   *Is anyone else likely to be affected?*
Other teams or departments.
The organization as a whole.
Other team leaders.
Do we need approval?

6   *What methods, techniques or actions shall we adopt?*
The teambuilding activities in the companion volume, *50
Activities for Teambuilding.*
Other activities and techniques known to me.
Other sources of ideas.

7   *What other resources will we need?*
Are we (or I) competent to undertake the activities?
Do we need external help?
Can other departments or teams help us?
Do we need to get out of the work situation?

8   *What time scale shall we adopt?*
1 month
1 year

9   *How shall we review progress?*
By self review.
By process observation.
By regular specific review meetings.
By other review methods contained in *50 Activities for
Teambuilding.*

10   *How will we assess whether further action is necessary?*
Should we evaluate our effect on others?
Should we analyse our needs again?

7 Groundrules for team development

People who have implemented teamwork improvement programmes generally have a great many 'war stories' to tell. Many mistakes have been made but from them it is possible to draw up some groundrules which should steer you away from many of the pitfalls and potential disaster areas. Most of them can be avoided if these simple rules are followed.

Start modestly. Remember that big oaks from little acorns grow and avoid grand designs. Success builds success and people will be much more committed to your ideas if they have seen some simple things bringing improvement. It is invariably better to start with a topic which can be easily grasped.

Be clear about your aims. It is often said that providing a group of intelligent individuals know what they want to achieve they will usually be capable of finding a way of achieving it. So often people seem to lose sight of the aim or become more concerned with the method than with the outcome.

Remember that the unknown is usually more threatening than the known. Hardy, the trusted companion of Lord Nelson, on leaving the sea took up a post at the Greenwich Naval College near London. The story is told of him as a local dignitary receiving an invitation to be a passenger on the first passenger railway train from Greenwich to Central London. Hardy, a man who had fought gallantly in some of the most bloody and horrendous sea battles in history, declined the invitation as 'he could see little point in exposing himself to the tremendous risks involved'.

Remember that development is basically self-regulated. Limitations are imposed by age, beliefs and capacity, and although you can create development opportunities ultimately individuals are responsible for their own development.

Remember those who have not had development opportunities. Successful development for some can mean jealousy from others who may feel aggrieved at not being part of the action.

Be alive to other opportunities which your actions may create. Working on teamwork issues will inevitably bring about opportunities to improve such things as individual development, the flow of ideas in the organization, etc., and as a team becomes more effective it will begin to challenge things such as the way you are organized, the salary system, recruitment policies. All of these can be either barriers to your success or opportunities for greater success. The wise leader uses opportunities well.

Ensure that you have the agreement of participants before you proceed. Commitment to change comes from real understanding of the process you are about to embark upon. It may seem on occasions that you have to spend three times as much energy explaining to people what it is you are about to do as on the action itself, but no changes will be beneficial in the long run if they lack the commitment of those whom they affect. Group decisions are more binding. They are also usually wiser.

Remember you can take a horse to water but you cannot make it drink. People cannot be forced into changing their attitudes. They need to make up their own minds about where they stand and about what seems right to them. Similarly, you cannot force people to be open and honest. You may be able to force them to pretend to be open and to say they are honest but no good will come from inducing people to act contrary to their beliefs.

Be ready to accept the need for external help on occasions. Whilst taking responsibility for your own actions and helping others to do the same, there are many advantages that can be gained by using an 'outsider' in your organization. If you choose wisely you can capitalize upon the advantages of impartiality and lack of vested interest by, for instance, inviting an observer to your everyday meetings. But do not be afraid to question your adviser's approach, experience and beliefs. Such action is likely to increase respect for you.

Learn from your mistakes. Always be ready to admit you are wrong and use your past experience as a guide to improve future action. This means regular reviewing of the targets you have set and encouraging others to do the same. Honest feedback is the most valuable thing which your colleagues can give to you but people will not give honest feedback if they think that it will not be welcomed and may be used against them.

Consult widely and genuinely. People really do have a useful contribution to make and having been consulted they will also feel more committed to the project. It is easy to look upon consultation as a chore, or as a subtle way of selling an idea, and many managers are well practised in the skill of persuading others. However, manipulation of this kind is likely to undermine any teambuilding effort.

Face up to 'political' or organizational problems. Every organization has its politics and its politicians and turning a blind eye to them will not make them go away. Try to recognize the political barriers at an early stage, take account of them in your plans and, if necessary, confront them squarely and openly. Above all do not play the political game yourself; this will only discredit you in the eyes of those you are trying to help.

Encourage frank discussions about principles and practice. Deep rooted prejudices, views and beliefs will only change if they are brought into the open and explored at length. Never stifle discussion, you will have a healthier organization if team members are accustomed to discussing matters of principle in a constructive way. Remember that you will be taking people into the unknown and everyone is naturally apprehensive about things they do not understand or which seem to herald major changes. In addition, as the team increases its skill and experience, it will become increasingly willing and able to deal with more difficult problems.

Keep your plans and actions related to the work of the organization. People are unlikely to experiment if that experimentation involves substantial extra work. One good way of adhering to this rule is to try to use meetings and current projects as the basis for any improvement. The more work related you can keep your plans the more people will be willing to try them and the easier it will be to see meaningful results.

Be realistic about time scales. Rome was not built in a day, and you are unlikely to see any overnight changes. The way in which people behave in organizations is often the result of a lifetime's learning and whenever older people embark on new organizational learning there is a lot of 'unlearning' which needs to accompany it. Change in the culture of an organization is something which is very difficult to achieve. It requires constant attention and must be spread over a realistic time scale.

Do not raise expectations which you cannot meet. It is easy to promise people that any activities you embark upon will bring wholesale benefits but both you and the designs will be discredited if those around you are able to see clearly that your schemes did not really succeed. It is therefore imperative to be alive to, and to face up to, organizational and political problems and to recognize that for every two steps forward which you take you may also have to take one backwards.

Delegate where appropriate. There may be particular development activities which you are not well suited to undertake. In these circumstances look around for others who may be better equipped, remembering that delegation itself is one of the best development opportunities you are likely to find.

Re-organize or re-allocate work when necessary. People cannot always cope with their existing responsibilities as well as development prospects.

Get to know your strengths and weaknesses. Only when the team has a clear perception of its strengths and weaknesses will it know what it can exploit and improve and what it must overcome to be more effective. A clear vision of things as they are now is the first step in the development process.

Get to know the threats and opportunities in the external environment. Whenever you want to achieve change there will be external forces working for you and against you. Analysing those forces and then taking steps to enhance the positive forces and lessen or eliminate the negative forces can greatly aid your development work.

Practise what you preach. You will be judged by your actions much more than by your words.

A final note of caution. Although your efforts may bring results, remember that your success can lead to problems for others in terms of

- improving the effectiveness of your team can make other, less productive groups feel insecure;
- people and teams can and do grow beyond the needs of their present roles;
- the new methods of working which your team will develop can

easily challenge the style and operation of the whole organization;

- jealousy and resentment can be created in those who have not been part of the action.

8 Designing teambuilding events

The material in this manual has been set out in a way which will enable those who wish to facilitate work on teambuilding to use it to design training and intervention programmes. For instance the theory included in Part III has been grouped into nine brief and concise sections in order that they can be easily used as 'inputs', 'handouts' or 'aides-mémoire'. Similarly the techniques, structured experiences, methods and questionnaires included in *50 Activities for Team-building* are presented in a format which enables them to be used by the facilitator in either a training session or an everyday work situation. In Part IV I have also tried as far as possible to link each of the activities with the theory, particularly by identifying those activities which can be used to explore further the various 'building blocks of effective teamwork'.

In order to help further those who wish to build up training or intervention designs a number of example designs have been included which I have personally used and which have been built up entirely from the contents of this manual or its companion volume. The designs are flexible and can be adjusted to suit different participants, problems and time scales. It is hoped that they will be useful in demonstrating the way in which the material can be used to build up training sessions. This can be done by using a set of simple guidelines, which, if followed, should be of great assistance in designing training events which are stimulating, meaningful and enjoyable.

GUIDELINES FOR DESIGNING TRAINING EVENTS

1   Always start by defining the objectives you wish to achieve.
2   Because teambuilding often depends on openness, members must be prepared to say what they really think. This means that participants must attend on a voluntary basis.
3   Allow adequate time. It is important that events should proceed until a natural conclusion is reached.
4   Notwithstanding the need to reach a natural conclusion establish a time table and keep to it as far as possible. Make sure that other facilitators or leaders understand the timings, but do not close down discussion prematurely.
5   Select activities and lecturettes which will best help you achieve the objectives.
6   As far as possible select and use activities which reinforce the points made in the lecturettes.
7   Try to intersperse activities, lecturettes and discussions to give a balanced programme.
8   Allow adequate time to discuss or process the activities.
9   Use only activities which you feel you can handle efficiently given the facilities and help which are available to you.
10 Try to start with an 'unfreezing' activity which will not be seen as threatening and will allow people to immediately begin participating in the event.
11 Try out activities with which you are not familiar *before* the event.
12 Ensure that adequate preparation is done before the event begins. In particular, check that answer sheet, copies of activities and visual aids are to hand.
13 Consider how structured you wish the event to be.

In the main, heavily structured events are easier to handle, particularly for managers and trainers who may be breaking new ground. Because of this they stand a greater chance of achieving their objectives, and of giving their participants a greater feeling of security.

In less structured events, where participants are given more opportunity to influence the content and style, there is greater scope for real and deep learning because participants are more likely to learn from their own participation. A more flexible design will give more options and freedom and allow participants to resolve issues which are peculiar to them.

However, greater skill is usually required from the trainer.

Often trainers build their experience and ability by moving from more to less structured events.

14   Try to eliminate jargon and difficult theory wherever possible.
15   Remember that most of the activities in *50 Activities for Teambuilding* are capable of amendment to satisfy your own particular requirements.
16   Try to avoid the threatening. Some teambuilding activities can be not only threatening but potentially damaging, particularly those which give direct and personal feedback. Where direct feedback is inevitable ensure counselling and support.
17   The event will have a greater chance of success if the participants have themselves been involved in defining the problem.

THE TRAINING DESIGNS

The different designs which can be derived from the material are almost endless. A few examples are given to show how the material can be arranged for different purposes, though not to suggest actual designs for use by the reader who is strongly advised to build up his own designs using the guidelines given earlier. Therefore, training designs which vary in objectives, in length and in participants have been purposely included.

1: Improving our teamwork. Originally designed as a 'starter' event to enable an existing team to explore the potential of, and need for, teambuilding. I have often used this design with teams who are considering teamwork for the first time and need a general introduction as a prelude to further work.

2: An introduction to team leadership issues. Designed to allow managers with no previous experience of teambuilding activities to begin examining their own role and behaviour in relation to the teams they are leading. Originally used with managers in a large organization who had previously received no formal training, it has been used since to whet the appetite of many managers.

3: An introduction to teamwork. An introduction to team development for people who do not regularly work together and wish to be introduced to its potential. Originally it was used for a large gathering of chief executives of retail stores groups who had heard about team development and wanted to know a little more.

4: Teamwork workshop. A medium length event enabling people to familiarize themselves with essential theory and activities as a prelude to understanding teambuilding activities in their own teams/ organizations. The design has been used on several occasions as the basis for public workshops where trainers and managers from different organizations come together for two to three days.

5: Improving my management of others. A full day in which managers can assess their performance as team leaders and make plans to improve their future performance. A step on from design 2 this can be used where managers are prepared to invest a full day in examining their own strengths and weaknesses. This design was originally put together for a group of managers, each of whom managed individual plants, who met together for an annual business conference and wished to spend part of the time examining how they managed their own units.

6: Depth teambuilding workshop. A one week event in which a team can work seriously on the fundamental issues which will improve its functioning and prepare plans for the future.

7: Understanding teamwork. A one day event for those who need to understand the theory of team development but who do not regularly work together. The design was originally used with a group of consultants who had little experience of teambuilding but were increasingly being asked by clients to advise on its potential.

EXAMPLE TRAINING DESIGN 1: IMPROVING OUR TEAMWORK

Objectives
To provide an opportunity for teams to understand:
(a)   The importance of teamwork.
(b)   Its relationship to other organizational problems.
(c)   The need for improvement.

Time required: Approximately 1 day.

Participants: Teams who regularly work together and have not previously been exposed to teambuilding theory or activities.

Programme Item	Approximate time required	Source
1 Input 'What is teamwork?' (preceded by Brainstorming)	50min	Part I Section 1 Activity 13
2 Distribution of 'Building blocks' questionnaire Completion of 'Building blocks' questionnaire (facilitator collects)	30 min	Part II Section 2
3 Activity 'Highway Code'	60 min	Activity 25
4 Review of performance in 'Highway Code' (Group discussion)	40 min	
LUNCH		
5 Activity 'Zin obelisk' followed by review	40 min	Activity 31
6 Input 'Stages of development'	30 min	Part I Section 3
7 Activity 'Our team and its stage of development'	30 min	Activity 1
8 Results of 'Building blocks' questionnaire presented by facilitator Discussion of results	50 min	
9 Input 'What teamwork will not do'	30 min	Part I Section 4

EXAMPLE TRAINING DESIGN 2: AN INTRODUCTION TO TEAM LEADERSHIP ISSUES

Objectives

To provide an opportunity for team leaders to:

(a) Question their assumptions and beliefs about the management of others.

(b) Examine their performance in working with others.

(c) Consider the theory of effective team leadership.

Time required: Approximately 4½ hours.

Participants: Anyone with responsibility for the leadership/management of teams.

Programme

Item	Source
1 *Our assumptions and beliefs* Completion of 'Team leadership style' questionnaire	Activity 7
Input 'Appropriate leadership'	Part III Building
Sharing of results and discussion	block 7
2 *Working with others* Task 1 'Zin obelisk'	Activity 31
Short lecture 'What makes teams effective'	Part I Section 2
Task 2 'Team rating'	Activity 3
Discussion of results	
Task 3 'My meetings with others'	Activity 9
3 The role of the team leader input – given as handout	Part I Section 5

EXAMPLE TRAINING DESIGN 3: AN INTRODUCTION TO TEAMWORK

Objectives

To provide a basic introduction to teamwork issues by:

(a)   Explaining *basic* teamwork theory.

(b)   Experiencing simple teamwork activities.

Time required: Approximately 3 hours.

Participants: Anyone who has not experienced teambuilding activities previously.

Programme

Item	Source
1 Input 'What is a team?'	Part I Section 1
2 Task 1 'Cave rescue'	Activity 27
3 Short lecture 'What is teamwork?'	Part I Section 2
4 Discussion – Teams review performance in Task 1 against 'Team self-review'	Activity 41
5 Task 2 'Highway Code'	Activity 25
6 Discussion – Teams review performance in Task 2 against 'Team self-review'	Activity 41

EXAMPLE TRAINING DESIGN 4: TEAMWORK WORKSHOP

Objectives
To provide a medium length training experience in which participants can:

(a) Explore the importance of effective teamwork.
(b) Understand basic teamwork theory.
(c) Consider particularly issues of balanced roles, management style, support and trust, co-operation and conflict.
(d) Receive practical guidance and ideas on assessing teamwork problems and beginning to improve teamwork.
(e) Develop action plans based on the above.

Time required: 2 days.

Participants: Key managers in organization.

Programme Item	Approximate time required	Source
Day 1		
1 Activity 'To see ourselves as others see us' and discussion of results	60 min	Activity 38
2 Activity 'Highway Code'	60 min	Activity 25
3 Input 'What is a team?' and 'What is teamwork?' (balanced roles, co-operation and conflict, support and trust, and appropriate leadership are identified as basis for rest of design)	45 min	Part I Sections 1 and 2
4 Syndicates review performance against criteria outlined	45 min	
LUNCH		
5 Input 'Co-operation and conflict'	10 min	Part III Building block 5
Activity 'Prisoner's dilemma' with	60 min	Activity 29
Activity 'Process review'	25 min	Activity 39

Programme

Day 1 Item	Approximate time required	Source
6 Input 'Support and trust'	10 min	Part III Building block 4
Activity 'Cave rescue'	45 min	Activity 27
Activity 'Team self-review'	25 min	Activity 41
7 Input 'Appropriate leadership'	10 min	Part III Building block 7
Activity 'Team leadership style'	40 min	Activity 7
8 Input 'The role of the team leader'	30 min	Part I Section 5

BREAK

9 Activity 'Human structure'	45 min	Activity 30
Activity 'Four letter words'	45 min	Activity 33
10 Input 'Balanced roles'	15 min	Part III Building block 1

Day 2

1 Input 'Individual development'	15 min	Part III Building block 9
Activity 'Characteristics of personal effectiveness'	20 min	Activity 8
Discussion of results in pairs	30 min	
2 Distribution and individual completion of 'Building blocks' questionnaire	25 min	Part II
3 Action planning: Participants prepare plans for improvement of teamwork in back home situation using (a) personal learning achieved in workshop, (b) other activities from *50 Activities for Teambuilding* (c) action planning theory	120 min	Part I Section 6
4 Teams present action plans	60 min	
5 Short lecture 'Groundrules for team development'	30 min	Part I Section 7

EXAMPLE TRAINING DESIGN 5:
IMPROVING MY MANAGEMENT OF OTHERS

Objectives
To provide an opportunity for team leaders to:
(a) Question their assumptions and beliefs about the management of others.
(b) Assess their personal performance in working with others.
(c) Obtain basic guidance on applying this learning in their own situation:

Time required: 1 day.

Participants: Managers who normally lead teams.

Programme

Item	Source
Pre-Course Reading – The role of the team leader	Part I Section 5
1 *My assumptions and beliefs about others*	
Completion of 'Management style: theory X–Y'	Activity 20
Input 'Appropriate, leadership'	Part III Building
Discussion on input content and results of questionnaire	block 7
2 *My performance in working with others*	
Activity 'The Zin obelisk'	Activity 31
Review of results (processors may be used) (or team self review)	Activity 39 or 41
Input 'What is teamwork?'	Part I Section 2
Activity 'My meetings with others'	Activity 9
3 *My performance as a coach*	
Activity 'How good a coach are you?'	Activity 17
4 *My overall performance*	
Activity 'Team leader effectiveness'	Activity 6
5 Action planning with	
(a) Groundrules for team development	Part I Section 7
(b) Action planning checklist	Part I Section 6
(c) 'Being a better coach'	Activity 18
(d) Group counselling by facilitator	

EXAMPLE TRAINING DESIGN 6: DEPTH
TEAMBUILDING WORKSHOP

Objectives

To provide an opportunity for team members to:

(a)   Understand the importance of teamwork.
(b)   Relate this to operational plans.
(c)   Analyse team development needs.
(d)   Prepare action plans for teamwork improvement.

Time required: 5 days.

Participants: Intact work group or leaders of a number of teams.

Programme

Day 1   Source

  1 Presentation of forward work-plans
    for organization or work group and
    agreement of them

Day 2 Understanding teamwork

  2 Activity 'Who are you?'   Activity 23
  3 Activity 'Highway Code'   Activity 25
  4 Input 'What is a team?'   Part I Section 1
    'Team self-review' briefing followed   Activity 41
    by review of performance in
    'Highway Code'
  5 Input 'Co-operation and conflict'   Part III Building
                                           block 5

    Activity 'Prisoner's dilemma'   Activity 29
    Activity 'Process review'   Activity 39
  6 Input 'Support and trust'   Part III Building
                                           block 4

  7 Activity 'Cave rescue'   Activity 27
    Activity 'Process review'   Activity 39
  8 Input 'Good communications'   Part III Building
                                           block 11

Day 3

  7 Input 'Appropriate leadership'   Part III Building
                                           block 7

Activity 'Management style: theory X–Y'	Activity 20
8 Activity 'Characteristics of personal effectiveness'	Activity 8
Input 'Individual development'	Part III Building
Teams discuss results of 'Characteristics of personal effectiveness'	block 9
9 Input 'Clear objectives'	Part III Building block 2
Activity 'Four letter words'	Activity 33
Input 'Good communications'	Part III Building block 11
10 Input 'Decision-making'	Part III Building block 6
Activity 'How we take decisions'	Activity 45

(In activities where process review is used members should take turns acting as observer. The facilitators may deliver a brief input on process review either in plenary session or repeated to each group of observers as they take turns.)

Day 4

11 Input 'The stages of team development'	Part I Section 3
Activity 'Our team and its stage of development'	Activity 1
12 Completion of 'Building blocks' questionnnaire	Part II
Input 'Building blocks of effective teamwork'	Part I Section 2
13 Discussion of results	
14 Input 'Action planning'	Part I Sections 6 and 7 (Action planning and Groundrules for team development)

Day 5 Action planning

15 Participants split into small groups to prepare actions plans for:
  (a) Individual development
  (b) Group development

Use as basis for planning:

(a) Results of
     'Characteristics of personal effectiveness'
     'Management style: Theory X–Y'
     Building blocks questionnaire
     'Our team and its stage of development'
(b) Discussions after each activity
     including 'Process review' and 'Team self-review'
(c) Copies of activities from *50 Activities for Teambuilding*,
     which are distributed

16 Plans of small groups presented to all participants
17 General discussion, comment on plans, and review of event

EXAMPLE TRAINING DESIGN 7: TEAMWORK ISSUES

Objectives
To promote understanding of Team development theory.

Time required: 1 day.

Participants: Groups of individuals who need to understand the basics.
They need not normally work together.

Programme Item	Approximate time required	Source
1 Pre-work – completion of Steps 1–4 'Team effectiveness action plan'		Activity 12
2 Input 'What is teamwork?'		Part I Section 2
Completion of 'Building blocks' questionnaire	25 min	Part II
3 Activity 'The Zin obelisk'	25 min	Activity 31
Review by 'Process review'	30 min	Activity 39
Discussion: The characteristics of effective teamwork	30 min	
4 Input 'The building blocks of effective teamwork'	25 min	Part III
Activity 'Intimacy exercise' (openness and confrontation)	30 min	Activity 24
Activity 'Silent shapes' (co-operation and conflict)	30 min	Activity 42
Review by 'Team self-review'	20 min	Activity 41
Activity 'Positive and negative feedback' (support and trust)	30 min	Activity 36
5 Scoring of 'Building blocks' questionnaire	20 min	
Activity 'Team rating'	25 min	Activity 3
6 Input 'Stages of team development'	15 min	Part I Section 3
Activity 'Our team and its stage of development'	20 min	Activity 1
7 Input 'Balanced roles and good communications'	30 min	Part III Building blocks 1 and 11
8 Completion of step 6 'Team effectiveness action plan'	30 min	Activity 12

PRINCIPLES OF ADULT LEARNING AND IMPLICATIONS FOR THE DESIGN OF TEAMBUILDING EVENTS

Following these guidelines will help improve your chances of success:

1 The participant is a partner in the learning experience and should be encouraged and given the opportunity to influence the learning design.

2 Adults, particularly those who occupy senior positions in organizations are very capable of taking responsibility for their own learning. Self directed learning activities can, therefore, be built into training event design.

3 Learning is enhanced when two-way communication takes place. Therefore avoid too many lecture sessions. Encourage designs which encourage a free exchange of ideas and insights between participants and trainers.

4 Adults will learn from reflecting on their own and other peoples' experiences. The use of interactive activities such as case studies, role playing and group activities will encourage reflection and learning.

5 What is perceived to be useful in everyday work situations will be learned; that which is perceived to have little reference to work or life situations will tend to be dismissed. It is therefore important that the learning design fit expressed and assessed needs. Try also to build in applications planning.

6 People expect to be treated with respect and learn best when they perceive that they are, being respected. It is therefore important to enquire about their problems and situations and demonstrate that due account is being taken of them.

7 Interest will determine attention and regular 'review' and 'process' activities will help ensure that interest is maintained.

8 Whilst highly structured and formal learning designs are often appropriate for young people, adults, particularly managers will resent this. They learn better in a climate which is personal and relatively informal. The degree of informality will need to reflect the degree of informality normally found within peer groups in the organization(s). 'Getting acquainted' and 'Interpersonal' activities help facilitate a more personal approach.

9 Adults are self-motivated to improve effectiveness but they filter learning through their own developed value systems. Activities

which focus on behavioural change and evaluation which is self directive will be helpful.

10   Learning is enhanced when participants are supported in experimenting with new ideas and skills. Support can be given by establishing 'home groups' where experiences can be shared and progress reviewed.

11   Adults are more set in their ways than children. Fixed points of view are often a barrier to new learning, so do not forget the necessity for 'unlearning'. Personal feedback activities and opportunities for experimentation will enhance 'unlearning'.

12   Adults will be more likely to apply that which they have had a part in planning. Thus modifying the event design both before and during the experience will give a greater sense of involvement and a greater likelihood of application.

PART II
DIAGNOSING TEAMWORK PROBLEMS

Debates about what constitutes an effective team can be endless but, as we saw in Part I, most such teams seem to exhibit a set of common characteristics, characteristics which are associated with the mature team. These were referred to as the building blocks of effective teamwork:

1 Balanced roles.
2 Clear objectives and agreed goals.
3 Openness and confrontation.
4 Support and trust.
5 Co-operation and conflict.
6 Sound procedures.
7 Appropriate leadership.
8 Regular review.
9 Individual development.
10 Sound inter-group relations.
11 Good communications.

The following questionnaire enables us to look at team strengths and weaknesses under each of these headings. Using it will start the process of diagnosing teamwork problems and of understanding more fully the concepts involved.

The building blocks questionnaire

This simple questionnaire has been developed as an aid to discovering which of the eleven building blocks of effective teamwork could be most useful to your team. It is a collection of statements which team members might be heard to make about affairs in their team and the more people in the team who complete it the more accurate will be the results.

It is important to ensure that those completing it share a common perception of the composition of the team under review, as of course, some may see themselves as belonging to more than one team.

Part IV 'Selecting teambuilding activities' indicates those particular activities which can be used for exploring and using the building blocks. With the help of this questionnaire you can, therefore, not only get a quick indication of which building blocks to use in your team but also be directed to those activities which will most easily start to make the team more effective.

Instructions for completion

1 Turn to the answer grid on p. 70.
2 Work through the statements, in numerical order and put a cross in the appropriate square of the grid if you think a statement about your team is broadly true. If you think a statement is not broadly true, leave the square blank.
3 Do not spend a great deal of time considering each statement; a few seconds should be long enough.

4 Remember that the results will be worthwhile only if you are truthful.

'BUILDING BLOCKS' QUESTIONNAIRE

1 Our team lacks leadership.
2 Decisions seem to be forced upon us.
3 People are not encouraged to speak out.
4 When the going gets tough it is every one for herself, or himself.
5 Communication needs improving.
6 Decisions are taken at the wrong level.
7 Some of the managers are not true to themselves.
8 We seldom question the content or usefulness of our meetings.
9 Insufficient development opportunities are created.
10 We are frequently at loggerheads with other departments.
11 Team members do not communicate with each other sufficiently.
12 The accepted order is rarely challenged.
13 No-one is really clear where we are going.
14 People do not say what they really think.
15 People have an 'I'm all right Jack' attitude.
16 Conflict is destructive in this team.
17 There is inadequate information on which to base decisions.
18 Some of the managers are not trusted.
19 We do not learn from our mistakes.
20 Managers do not help their subordinates to learn.
21 Relationships with other groups are 'cool'.
22 We do not project our position well within the organization.
23 We often find that we lack the required expertise.
24 We are all very busy but we do not seem to get anywhere.
25 Issues are brushed under the carpet.
26 It would help if people were more willing to admit their mistakes.
27 There is mistrust and hostility.
28 People are uncommitted to decisions.
29 There is little team loyalty.
30 Outside opinions are unwelcome.
31 There should be more job rotation.
32 We seldom work effectively with other teams.
33 We fail to secure co-operation from other teams or departments.

34 No-one builds the necessary bridges with other groups.

35 We do not spend adequate time planning for the future.

36 Delicate issues are avoided.

37 People get 'stabbed in the back'.

38 We do not really work together.

39 Inappropriate people make the decisions.

40 Managers are weak and not prepared to stand up and be counted.

41 I do not receive sufficient feedback.

42 The wrong kinds of skills are developed.

43 Help is not forthcoming from other parts of the organization.

44 There is a great deal of misunderstanding between our team and the trades unions who impact upon us.

45 We do not pay sufficient attention to relationships.

46 We do not have a clear view of what is expected of us.

47 Honesty is not a feature of our team.

48 I do not feel strengthened by my colleagues.

49 Skills and information are not shared sufficiently.

50 It is the strong personalities that get their own way.

51 Dignity is not recognized.

52 We should spend more time questioning the way we operate.

53 Managers do not take personal development seriously.

54 The rest of the organization does not understand us.

55 We fail to get our message over to the outside world.

56 We often reach decisions far too quickly.

57 The way an individual is valued has little to do with what is achieved.

58 There are too many secrets.

59 Conflicts are avoided.

60 Disagreements fester.

61 Commitment to decision is low.

62 Our manager(s) believe(s) that tighter supervision improves results.

63 There are too many taboos in this team.

64 There are manifestly better opportunities in other departments.

65 We put a lot of energy into defending our boundaries.

66 Team members do not understand what is expected of them.

67 We do not pay sufficient attention to new ideas.

68 Priorities are unclear.

69 People are not involved sufficiently in decision-making.

70 There are too many recriminations.

71   There is not enough listening.
72   We do not utilize the skills we have available.
73   Managers believe that people are inherently lazy.
74   We spend too much time doing and not enough thinking.
75   Individuals are not encouraged to grow.
76   We do not try to understand the views of other teams.
77   We fail to listen to our customers.
78   We tend to move before reaching conclusions.
79   We do not understand what other departments are aiming at.
80   Some people back down too easily.
81   Generally there is low trust here.
82   People are unwilling to take the views of others into account.
83   We do not consider alternative solutions sufficiently.
84   Yesterday's attitudes prevail with our manager(s).
85   The accepted order is rarely challenged.
86   Our manager(s) lack(s) the skills to develop others.
87   We have too little influence on the rest of the organization.
88   We could really use some training on how to improve communications.
89   We have too many specialists in our team.
90   Managers do not plan for the future together.
91   In this team it pays to keep your mouth shut.
92   A lot of time is spent 'defining' territory.
93   There are too many fights.
94   People feel frustrated because they are not consulted.
95   Management does not care whether people are happy in their work.
96   We seldom change our working procedures or organization.
97   We should spend more time developing our own senior people.
98   We do not reach out to help other groups.
99   The left hand doesn't know what the right hand is doing
100 We are not sufficiently results orientated.
101 Different parts of the organization are pulling in different directions.
102 People are not prepared to put their true beliefs forward.
103 People are not really helped to develop.
104 This place reminds me of a battlefield sometimes.
105 There is a need for more democracy.
106 Managers take little action to make employees' jobs interesting and meaningful.
107 Delicate issues are not raised.

108 Many people trained by the company later join competitors.
109 Ideas from outside the team are not used.
110 We lack the information we need to do the job.
111 We pay too little attention to the quality of our work.
112 Our aims are not democratically agreed.
113 Team members do not get sufficient honest feedback.
114 People should stand on their own feet more.
115 We should discuss our differences more.
116 Team members are not sufficiently involved in taking decisions.
117 Our leader does not make the best use of us.
118 We should seriously consider the relevance of our meetings.
119 Individual development is stifled by the team.
120 Information does not flow freely enough between teams.
121 Good ideas do not reach those who could implement them.
122 We have too many people with similar skills.
123 We should place more emphasis on results.
124 People 'hear what they want to hear' rather than the truth.
125 More time should be devoted to discussing fundamental values.
126 We do not get down to the root of our differences.
127 Decisions are taken at the wrong level.
128 Our leader is not true to his own beliefs.
129 We should take more account of how others see us.
130 People are discouraged from being authentic.
131 The organization as a whole is not a happy place to work in.
132 There is too little 'listening'.

BUILDING BLOCKS' ANSWER SHEET

Follow the instructions given at the beginning of the questionnaire. In the grid there are 132 squares, each one numbered to correspond to a question. Fill in the top line first, working from left to right; then fill in the second and subsequent lines. Be careful not to miss a question.

A	B	C	D	E	F	G	H	I	J	K
1	2	3	4	5	6	7	8	9	10	11
12	13	14	15	16	17	18	19	20	21	22
23	24	25	26	27	28	29	30	31	32	33
34	35	36	37	38	39	40	41	42	43	44
45	46	47	48	49	50	51	52	53	54	55
56	57	58	59	60	61	62	63	64	65	66
67	68	69	70	71	72	73	74	75	76	77
78	79	80	81	82	83	84	85	86	87	88
89	90	91	92	93	94	95	96	97	98	99
100	101	102	103	104	105	106	107	108	109	110
111	112	113	114	115	116	117	118	119	120	121
122	123	124	125	126	127	128	129	130	131	132

Totals

When you have considered all 132 statements, total the number of crosses in each vertical column and turn to the next page.

Now write the score for each column here. This is your score for

A ☐   Balanced roles

B ☐   Clear objectives and agreed goals

C ☐   Openness and confrontation

D ☐   Support and trust

E ☐   Co-operation and conflict

F ☐   Sound procedures

G ☐   Appropriate leadership

H ☐   Regular review

I ☐   Individual development

J ☐   Sound inter-group relations

K ☐   Good communications

The building blocks with the highest scores are the ones which you could probably use most profitably to bring improvements to your team. In Part III there is a section on each one of these building blocks which will explain it in greater depth. Before undertaking any team development activity you should study those which relate to your highest scoring blocks. At the end of Part IV there is a key which links the building blocks to practical activities in *50 Activities for Teambuilding*. By using it you can select those teambuilding activities which are appropriate to your team now.

However, before you rush to try them, look again through the sections in Part I. This will help you avoid many of the pitfalls and barriers you could easily come across.

PART III
THE BUILDING BLOCKS OF EFFECTIVE TEAMWORK

THE BUILDING BLOCKS

In writing about 'The building blocks of effective teamwork' I have had in mind the following uses for the material:

1   To explain further the 'Building blocks' of effective teamwork described earlier.
2   To provide notes which the manager/trainer can use to give 'inputs' on training/educational events.
3   To help explain and discuss the outcomes of teambuilding activities, particularly when they are used in 'workshop' situations.
4   Theoretical reading for those who wish to understand some of the concepts of team development.
5   'Hand-out' material before, during or after training sessions.
6   Follow-up reading or discussion material after using the building blocks questionnaire.
7   To help explain the implications of teambuilding to senior management.

One section is allocated to each of the 'building blocks':

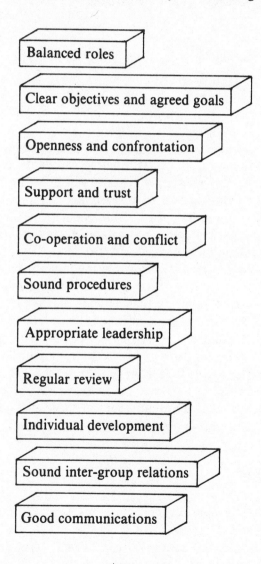

Balanced roles

Clear objectives and agreed goals

Openness and confrontation

Support and trust

Co-operation and conflict

Sound procedures

Appropriate leadership

Regular review

Individual development

Sound inter-group relations

Good communications

Building block 1: Balanced roles

One of the great strengths of the effective team lies in its blend of different talents and abilities. Truly effective teams are able to use different personalities and approaches to suit differing situations but they can only do this if the mix of team membership is right: if it is balanced. Too often work teams are formed without any conscious effort to ensure that membership is balanced; but senior managers are increasingly realizing that it is worth the effort. Good teambuilding has to begin with good selection. Just as the master chef has to choose between ingredients, ensure their quality and determine the correct quantities, so the teambuilder has to find the optimum balance of skills and abilities. Some people may be fully trained in the skills they offer whilst others may be developing. Some may have the wisdom of the years on their side, others the vigour of youth but all must contribute to the whole and a balance must be achieved. Recent research has enabled us to understand why teams succeed or fail, by analysing the roles which are necessary in successful teams. Each of the following roles has its unique contribution to make.

THE LEADER

All teams need a leader, although different members may assume the role of leader in different situations. At the outset, the leader's job is to form the team, to identify strengths and weaknesses, and to determine contributions. Objectives must be set and performance monitored. Meetings will be called and a structure provided for them. The main role of the leader is to get the best out of everyone and to review the different needs of the team at different stages of its development and for differing tasks.

THE CHALLENGER

Often seen as the 'Maverick' of the team as s/he often adopts an unconventional approach. This is an individual who will look afresh at what the team is doing and why and who will challenge the accepted order. Because of this, such an individual is often unpopular with those who prefer to conform and can be accused of 'rocking the boat'. The challenger provides the unexpected and whilst many ideas may prove to be worthless, some may become 'the idea of the year'. Without a challenger the team can become complacent for it lacks the stimulus to review radically what the team is doing and how it is doing it.

THE EXPERT

We live in an age of ever increasing specialization and the team may require several specialists whose primary role is to provide expertise which is not otherwise available to the team. Outside their area of specialization, these people make little contribution; in meetings they assume the role of 'expert witness' giving a professional viewpoint which the rest of the team may need to evaluate in the light of other constraints and opportunities. The expert may be an accountant, engineer, marketing adviser, trainer, personnel specialist, corporate planner or any other specialist, whose primary role is to provide the team with the expertise required to meet a particular objective.

THE AMBASSADOR

Like ambassadors who represent governments overseas, the ambassador in a team 'goes abroad' and builds the external relationships which enable the team to complete its task. An outgoing personality who makes friends easily, this is the public relations representative who tests the environment in which the team operates: a salesperson and a bridge builder who makes connections and knows the right people.

THE JUDGE

Like the judge in the courtroom this team member listens, questions and ponders before making a decision. This character tends to keep out of the arguments and does not see himself or herself as an advocate for any particular view or cause, but is concerned to see that ideas are properly evaluated and that the right decisions are made

A judge will not be rushed, preferring to pay the price of slow progress to make sure that the team follows the right path. Down to earth and logical, regarded by some as slow and ponderous, this person provides a balance and a check on those who may be carried away by their own enthusiasm; like the courtroom judge seeking out the truth and seeing justice done.

THE INNOVATOR

Here is one who uses imagination to the full: an ideas person who is always proposing new ways of doing things. The innovator ensures that new ideas are evaluated, nurtured and developed and builds on the original ideas of others, visualizing opportunities and transforming ideas into practical strategies. A fearless capacity to grapple with complex problems which demand new approaches provides the team with a rich resource of vision, ingenuity, imagination and logic and can usually help the team to understand the unconventional and the new.

THE DIPLOMAT

The diplomat is the team member who knows the diplomatic solution. This character generally has high influence within the team and is a good negotiator, and because of these skills plays a large part in orientating the team towards successful outcomes. Building alliances within and outside the team and trying to ensure that solutions are acceptable to all, the diplomat can sometimes be accused of 'papering over the cracks' in an effort to compromise, but is often dealing with the 'Art of the possible' rather than the ideal solution. Ways are found through difficult problems and in difficult times this is often the person who leads the team through dangerous ground.

THE CONFORMER

Helping in every way and always to be relied upon to fill the inevitable gap that no-one had thought of, the conformer adopts a co-operative stance and so helps the others to feel at ease. This character seldom challenges authority, rarely rocks the boat, preferring to use time and skills to good effect. Often the team's odd job person who may not have any outstanding expertise, but who observes what is happening and what is needed and then uses a breadth of experience to its best advantage. Invaluable as a 'fixer', he or she works for the good of the company and is generally conservative in outlook.

THE OUTPUT PUSHER

A self motivated achiever with persistent drive to see tangible results, this is the team's target person who reminds everyone about time scales and output requirements, who acts as the progress chaser and ensures that the team 'gets to its target'. He or she has high task commitment and this can rub off on others ensuring a more results orientated operation. This character is often intolerant of the views and problems of other team members and can be abrasive in approach.

THE QUALITY CONTROLLER

Here is a check on the 'output orientation' of the Output Pusher. The quality controller is often heard to remark 'if a job is worth doing it is worth doing well'. Quality is the watchword. This is the person who inspires the team to strive for higher standards, who can be accused of holding up progress and who may often clash with the Output Pusher in the desire to see that quality is maintained. Here is the conscience of the team, upholding concern for the quality of relationships, services and leadership as well as the product.

THE SUPPORTER

The supporter makes people feel at ease and builds morale within the team. This character is strongly relationships orientated seeking to

Roles summary sheet

Team leader
Forms the team
Identifies strengths and
weaknesses
Determines contributions
Sets objections
Monitors performance
Calls meetings
Provides structure
Reviews team needs

Challenger
Adopts unconventional
approaches
Looks afresh
Challenges accepted
order
Provides the unexpected
Ideas person
Challenges complacency
Provides stimulus
Promotes radical review

Expert
Provides specialist expertise
Acts as an expert witness
Provides professional viewpoint

Ambassador
Develops external
relationships
Shows concern for external
environment
Sells the team
Builds bridges

Judge
Listens
Evaluates
Ponders
Avoids arguments
Avoids advocacy
Promotes justice
Avoids rushing
Acts logically
Acts pragmatically
Provides balance
Checks wild enthusiasm
Seeks the truth

Innovator
Uses imagination
Progresses new methods
Evaluates ideas
Motivates others
Builds on others ideas
Visualizes opportunities
Transforms ideas into strategies
Deals with complex issues
Provides vision
Provides ingenuity
Provides logic
Helps understanding

Diplomat
Promotes diplomatic solutions
Has high influence
Good negotiator
Orientates the team
Builds alliances
Aids consensus
Pragmatic
Sees way ahead

Conformer
Fills gaps
Co-operative
Helps relationships
Jack of all trades
Avoids challenges to
accepted order
Observes
Conservative

Output Pusher
Self motivated
Pre-occupation with output and
results
Drives
Imposes time scale
Checks progress
Shows high commitment to task
Intolerant
Abrasive

Quality controller
Checks output orientation
Preoccupation with quality
Inspires higher standards
Acts as team conscience
Shows relationship concern

Supporter
Builds morale
Puts people at ease
Ensures job satisfaction
Resolves conflicts
Gets to root of
problem
Gives advice
Supports
Encourages

Reviewer
Observes
Reviews performance
Promotes regular review
Gives feedback
Acts as mirror
Looks for pitfalls
Is process orientated

ensure that the right conditions are created for people to give of their best and derive satisfaction from their working life. The supporter takes a lead in resolving conflict within the group but prefers to get to the root of the problem rather than paper over the cracks. Others feel that they can turn to the supporter for advice. This member of the team supports and encourages and hence is a considerable help in developing the contributions of others.

THE REVIEWER

Full of objective observations about the way in which the team is operating, this character helps the team to perform better in the future by reviewing past performance. Because it is easier to observe from outside whilst not taking part in the task, part of this role on occasions can be given to an external consultant who specializes in 'process review'. However, this is not a substitute for the regular internal review which is a hallmark of highly successful teams. The reviewer gives feedback to the team, acting as a mirror and enabling the team to see itself, looks for pitfalls and continually considers the way in which the group operates, tends to be a sceptic and is 'process' rather than 'task' or 'relationships' orientated.

Remember that each of the above is a role and not an individual member. Some individuals may act almost exclusively in one of the roles but others may represent a blend of roles. Perhaps the most useful member of any team is the one who can adopt different roles in different situations. Obviously the smaller the team the more roles it is necessary for each member to play.

Building block 2: Clear objectives and agreed goals

No group of people is likely to be effective unless it knows what it wants to achieve. As a West Country friend often remarks 'People need to know where they be to'. The first step in achievement is usually realizing what it is we want to achieve; usually an intelligent group of people is capable of devising its own methods providing the members are clear on the desired outcome. But having clear objectives and agreed goals is more than just knowing what the outcomes need to be. People are only likely to be committed to objectives if they also feel some identity with and ownership for them, in other words if objectives and goals are discussed and agreed by team members. Often this agreement is difficult to achieve but experience tells us that it is an essential prerequisite of the effective team and that hence it is worth a great deal of trouble to get it right.

All organizations and teams exist for a purpose and yet so often the way in which they operate demonstrates that the purpose is unclear. If a team has no clear view of what it wants to achieve, then it necessarily follows that individuals cannot contribute in any optimum way towards its success. Even where team objectives are understood and agreed there is still often a gap between team and personal objectives. One of the chief indicators of effective team working is that this gap has been narrowed as much as possible. This means that effective teams must recognize both personal and group needs. The need for fulfilment, recognition and achievement, for instance, may be very strong in individuals and some people may be quite unhappy in a team unless these individual needs are being met.

The effective team allows individual members to give of their best and to take from the team those things which they need. Trying to make people the same will not bring about effectiveness.

Some of the main barriers to achieving clear objectives and agreed goals are:

1   The tendency for performance to be judged by input rather than output. In other words, we often measure people by the way they act and the things they do rather than the results they achieve at the end of the day. In organizations the world over, people are judged by how smart their dress is, whether they arrive at work on time, whether their desk is tidy, whether they make quick decisions and whether they are polite. In job descriptions we find phrases such as 'To organize', 'To report', 'To co-ordinate', 'To administer', rather than phrases which describe the results which are required. This is one of the principal reasons why job descriptions often become straitjackets.

2   Managers and subordinates not sharing a clear understanding of what is expected. This leads to wrong assumptions about the subordinate's ability and implies different standards on both sides. This problem has been the stumbling block of many so-called performance appraisal schemes.

3   Too often we consider how to achieve a task without really considering whether we should be performing that task at all. One simple test is to confront every task with the word 'why' and to keep asking that question until a satisfactory result is obtained. Only when the question 'why' has been satisfactorily answered should the question 'how' be asked.

Often the system used for monitoring results is inappropriate. One of the best examples I know was that of a team of Government sponsored consultants. They had difficult assignments which demanded considerable initiative, flair and experimentation, and yet they were judged on such things as the number of hours worked and correct completion of administrative forms. No serious attempt was ever made to assess their effectiveness from the clients' viewpoint and, in time, some of them began to see the completion of forms as more important than their clients' needs. 'The system must suit the needs of the business' *not* 'the business suits the needs of the system'.

Often people confuse 'winning' with achieving objectives. Most people, if they see themselves in a competitive situation, exhibit a desire to win and sometimes this can be quite counter-productive. People are rarely motivated by being beaten.

In order to overcome some of these problems, organizations have introduced elaborate systems and given them names like strategic planning, corporate planning, performance review, and appraisal. Perhaps the most widely used and known is management by objectives and the basis of this is joint agreement on the results which can reasonably be expected, the time it should take and the methods to be used for assessing results. Experience has shown that such formal schemes are of most benefit where people have to work on their own initiative or without close support or in isolated locations. They are less beneficial where people have regular contact with colleagues, work under close supervision or have largely repetitive jobs.

Here are a few rules about setting objectives.

1 If objectives are to provide a useful aid to motivation then they need to be democratically conceived.
2 Managers, teams and individuals need to be involved in determining their own areas of responsibility and their own objectives.
3 The emphasis should be on 'results to be achieved' rather than 'things to do'.
4 Managers and subordinates must agree on results required, methods of measuring them, and a timetable for review.
5 The changing environment must be kept in mind throughout.
6 Objectives should as far as possible be (a) specific, (b) time bounded, (c) measurable.

Greater motivation, fewer demands on management, less conflict, greater creativity and initiative, less need for punishments and threats, and better use of time and energy are just some of the advantages which come from clear objectives and agreed goals.

One final point to remember is that organizational as well as team and individual objectives need to change. There are countless examples of organizations who may have been clear about objectives in the beginning, but have paid the price of not reviewing them with the passing years. The organization which looks ahead, foresees difficulties, seizes opportunities and learns to redefine its aims in the light of changing circumstances is the one that ultimately succeeds.

Building block 3: Openness and confrontation

If a team is to be effective then the members of it need to be able to state their views, their differences of opinion, interests and problems without fear of ridicule or retaliation. No teams work really effectively if there is a 'cut-your-throat' or 'stabbing-in-the-back' atmosphere. Where members become less willing or able to express themselves openly much energy, effort and creativity are lost. Similarly there is a need to confront problems and issues rather than avoid them. Effective teams do not avoid delicate or unpleasant issues, they confront them honestly and squarely.

Thus two of the hallmarks of good teamwork are openness and confrontation. They are the attributes which often separate objective, sound teamwork from the shallow charade which passes for teamwork. In many organizations because openness and confrontation are manifestations of both attitude and behaviour, they are slow to appear and difficult to teach, and in most cases are a result of long and diligent teambuilding activities. What we do know is that openness and confrontation improve as the following circumstances come about.

IMPROVEMENT IN COMMUNICATION AND FEEDBACK

As communication between members of a team improves, so openness and confrontation develop. Real communication is candid and honest, and is concerned with genuine understanding and sharing of feelings and experiences. The type of communication which tells others only part of the truth inhibits openness and does not advance teamwork. Crucial to this is the feedback we give to and receive from others. Feedback is generally most helpful where:

(a) it takes into account the needs of the receiver (and the giver) at that point in time;
(b) it concentrates on describing events or feelings rather than evaluating them;
(c) it concentrates on things which the receiver can do something about;
(d) it is as specific as possible;
(e) it is timed to be near to the event and at a time when the receiver is receptive to it;
(f) understanding of it is checked.

INCREASE IN SELF-KNOWLEDGE

As individuals, through teambuilding activities, begin to know themselves better, to know their colleagues better, and to build one-to-one and one-to-all relationships, they find that openness and confrontation also develop. Honest self-knowledge recognizes true weaknesses and strengths and admits them to others, so that help can be offered and obtained. Requesting and obtaining help increases mutual understanding and respect amongst team members and fosters genuine openness.

CONSTRUCTIVE USE OF CONFLICT

Conflict, properly managed and constructively employed, leads to greater understanding amongst members of a team. Positive conflict, which deals in facts and is intended to help individuals or the team to improve by talking through problems until sound understanding is reached, encourages both openness and trust. Negative conflict, which relies on rumour and opinion, and is intended to wound and divide, breeds mistrust and hostility.

INCREASE IN ACTIVE LISTENING

Although listening is an aspect of good communication it needs emphasis. In good teams, listening involves more than merely hearing words. It demands a willingness to meet others half-way, and to forget personal feelings while considering others' views. Above all it demands a definite desire to understand the attitude and feelings of the speaker and what he is really trying to say. Active listening can increase when we can:

(a) stop evaluating what we hear as we hear it;
(b) start putting to the back of our minds what we want to say in favour of the speaker;
(c) start 'parking' other things which are on our minds;
(d) stop looking around or being distracted;
(e) stop filtering the information so that we hear what we want to hear.

Openness and confrontation amongst team members also encourages greater creativity. They are not 'soft options', nor are they superficial values, although they are easily simulated for a short time.

Building block 4: Support and trust

Support and trust naturally go together for without one the other cannot exist. Both can best be achieved where individual team members do not feel they have to protect their territory or function, and feel able to talk straight to other team members about both nice and nasty things. With trust people can talk freely about their fears and problems and receive from others the help which they need to be more effective.

One definition of support is 'to strengthen by assistance'. It is an essential ingredient of an effective team. Support is often confused with sympathy, but the idea that support strengthens means the two are very different expressions of emotion. The sympathetic offering of a shoulder to weep or shower complaints on is not necessarily supportive, and in fact can have a weakening effect on relationships.

People, whether in a family or a firm will never be able to feel frank and open unless they also feel that other members are equally frank and open. Conflict avoided in the name of support is like building relationships on sand. It is also important that people working or living together sense that their shortcomings or mistakes will be accepted along with their strengths and weaknesses, if a healthy, supportive climate is to exist.

Business life involves people in many complex relationships with others. The simple diagram overleaf gives just a small picture of the possible and actual relationships in an organization.

For all of these relationships to be supportive, self and group perceptions need to be clear. One of the problems in achieving

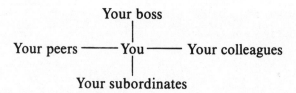

Your boss

Your peers ——— You ——— Your colleagues

Your subordinates

support is often that people's differing backgrounds, values and expectations colour perceptions to such an extent that communication
is not reached and support is not possible.

A second factor inhibiting support is competition over 'territory'.
People often feel very possessive and defensive over their areas of
responsibility, even about the information they have. Access to
information can mean power and a developing subordinate can often
be seen by an unsupportive boss as a territorial threat.

A third inhibiting factor is the imposition of, rather than the
agreement of goals and performance standards. Support between two
people has to be two-way and must be built on a relationship of trust
and mutual confidence. It is all too easy for this to be broken by
actions or attitudes perceived as domineering, patronizing or
condescending, and people often feel undermined when they are given
targets which have been set with little or no reference to them.

Perhaps the biggest single barrier to support is a low level of trust.
Trust takes a long time to achieve but it can be destroyed in a few
seconds. You cannot order others to trust you; it only comes through
their experience of you and it is perhaps the most difficult thing of all
to give through training. Trust is a belief that words will be translated
into action and that others will take your interest into account.

When these inhibiting factors have been overcome, it is possible to
create a supportive climate in which people can begin to move
towards agreed objectives and support each other with constructive
criticism, mutual confidence and frank, direct communications.
When people in a team really trust each other true support can be
experienced, support which strengthens not confirms weakness.

- *Honest dealing*   Those who go behind peoples' backs and who
  'talk with a forked tongue' are eventually found out. Managers
  who are seen as dealing dishonestly will find it almost impossible
  to engender trust.
- *Pragmatism*   Management is the 'art of the possible' and
  managers who find ways of making things happen in spite of

difficulties rather than sticking to 'ivory tower' solutions are more likely to be trusted.

- *Predictability* People find it hard to give their trust to managers who are changeable and incompetent. Predictability and order leads people to feel more compatible, and comfortable people find it easier to trust.
- *Loyalty* The leader who supports her or his followers through thick and thin is more likely to be trusted. Whilst recriminations may be necessary internally the team leader almost invariably needs to defend his team publicly if s/he is to enjoy their trust.

Support makes people feel wanted.

The leader's role in providing support is unique, the leader is the parent figure of the team whom members will watch and from whom they will take their lead. The leader's support is usually felt to be more valuable than that of other team members. Leaders can give support by listening, praising, appreciating, encouraging and dealing with issues which team members perceive as being real and important. As teams progress through the stages of team development, they require less support.

Building block 5: Co-operation and conflict

Co-operation means working together or, as defined by one dictionary, 'working together to share the profits'. Perhaps this is the essence of teamwork – that people put the team's objectives before their own and share both the financial and psychological rewards of their efforts. Co-operation implies that individuals are committed and willing to be involved in the work they do, and that they are ready to share their skills and information with the rest of the team, knowing that the others will reciprocate. People trust each other and encourage others to use their ideas. Everyone in the team is open about their strengths and weaknesses, knowing that they are accepted. This in itself places a great responsibility on the team to foster and maintain the spirit of co-operation and one finds that the members of the team remind and help individuals who may be falling behind with some task.

Co-operation implies that individuals trust other members' ability to consider their interests equally with their own and are willing for people to undertake assignments that contribute to the group's objectives. People are less suspicious of individuals' motives in carrying out important assignments.

Without trust and openness co-operation cannot occur. It is essential that people are able to talk frankly and without fear of looking foolish. The group leader and members need to work hard at achieving co-operation, for without it there is no real teamwork.

When there is a co-operative atmosphere members are more ready to be involved and committed, and information is shared rather than hidden. Individuals listen to the ideas of others and build on them. People find ways of being more helpful to each other and the team. Co-operation encourages high morale – individuals accept each others' strengths and weaknesses and contribute from their pool of knowledge and skills. All abilities, knowledge and experience are fully utilized by the team and individuals have no inhibitions about using other people's abilities to help with their problems. Problems are shared.

Where true co-operation is alive a degree of conflict is also seen as a necessary and useful part of organizational life. The effective team works through issues of conflict and uses the result to help achieve objectives. Conflict is so often seen as the opposite of co-operation. It is true that if a group of people are in constant disagreement they will find achievement difficult, but a certain amount of conflict also prevents a team becoming complacent and lazy and often is the source of new ideas. Traditionally, conflict has been seen as something caused by trouble makers or 'prima donnas' and something which by definition can be avoided or stifled. A more enlightened approach to conflict suggests that it is inevitable and an integral part of the process of change. If this is true, the management of conflict should be an aid to co-operation, not an obstacle. However, there are two sides to conflict. One is destructive and unhealthy, the other constructive and healthy. Destructive conflict, which defeats co-operation, can occur when individuals' carefully built images are threatened, when personalities intrude, when conflict is expected and the expectation becomes self-fulfilling or when two parties are arguing about different things without realizing it. Constructive, healthy conflict has a problem solving base. Those involved in solving the problems are willing to sublimate personality differences, to listen to others' views, to be open and candid to each other, to be supportive and helpful. With such behaviour, not only is each problem solved with total commitment, but subsequent team interaction becomes more effective, and co-operation improves.

Resolving unhelpful conflict means;

(a) examining what is causing trouble between people or groups;
(b) bringing the parties together to discuss the issues involved and to analyse their constituents;
(c) clarifying expectations and roles;
(d) learning how to utilize constructive feedback and value openness;
(e) learning how and when third parties can be helpful;
(f) reaching agreements about future action.

Building block 6: Sound procedures

The effective team thinks results first and methods second but also realises that sound working methods and decision-making lead to achievement of objectives. But, of course, objectives need to be clearly and completely understood by all team members before good decision-making can commence. Clarifying objectives is essential as it can prevent all the misunderstandings and defensive arguments that result from some people not knowing what is happening. In making decisions, good teams develop the ability to collect information quickly and then discuss the alternatives openly. They then become committed to their decisions and ensure that action ensues quickly.

Issues to consider are:

1   How is decision-making accomplished?
(a)   Is it mainly formal or informal?
(b)   At what levels are decisions taken?
(c)   Are people who will be affected really involved?
(d)   Is information collected properly and by the proper people?
(e)   Do people have the right information?
(f)   Is gossip used?
(g)   Do power groups operate, and if so are they harmful?
2   How are decisions implemented?
(a)   Do those who make decisions give the necessary authority for others to implement them?
(b)   Are decisions communicated effectively?
(c)   Are the right resources available and present?

(d) Are resources co-ordinated?
(e) Are people resistant to change, and if so how should we overcome this?
3   How are decisions reviewed?
(a) Who carries out the review?
(b) How often is it carried out?
(c) Does review really change things?

Decision-making is one of the basic processes involved in any manager's job; yet it is a process which is so often badly done, for example, at the wrong level in the organization with incomplete information, or carried out by people remote from the decision and thus not committed to it. To arrive at good decisions a flexible and explicit working procedure must exist which all members understand and adhere to.

The manager or team leader is the key man in determining the degree to which a team will participate in decision-making. There are four decision-making approaches which a leader can use. No leader could use one approach all of the time but the important thing is which of them is the preferred approach and which does he seek to utilize when circumstances allow.

1   *'I make the decisions around here.'* The leader solves the problem without asking the opinions of others or giving them an opportunity to contribute.
2   *'I will seek your opinion before I decide.'* The leader still makes the decision but based on opinions and information which he solicits from team members.
3   *'I take decisions with people of my choice.'* Here the leader takes decisions with certain team members whom he selects.
4   *'We take the decisions.'* Here the leader brings the problem before the team who discuss it and together they take the decision. The team may 'delegate' the decisions to an individual or subgroup if they consider that appropriate.

Perhaps the first question is: 'Are decisions being made in the right place in the organization?' In other words, are they being made at the right level, are they our decisions or do they belong to someone else? This needs to be considered both in terms of available and accurate information and whether the decision-making process helps to motivate the people who have to carry out the action resulting from it.

Effective decision-making by teams must rest upon a general consensus of agreement that the decision is a good one. It is not, however, merely a compromise since individuals are not afraid to disagree, and are listened to carefully.

Effective teams decide what information is needed, and allocate the collection of this to the most appropriate members. In order to do this roles and relationships must be clearly understood. This information is then openly and frankly discussed. Members are aware of their own values and those of people in the organization; they recognize the bias and prejudice that these values can have on decisions. They take into account the consequences of alternative decisions for departments, the organization, individuals, customers and suppliers, etc. When the decision is made there is commitment to it and the team ensures that action follows. Plans are made for implementation, again using the team's knowledge and skills as effectively as possible, and the resultant action is closely watched. People care about the quality of the decisions and are willing to learn from its consequences. They are also willing to modify the implementation if it does not seem to be working out.

To sum up, there are five main stages in effective decision-making:

1   A clear understanding of the reasons for taking a decision, i.e. the problem or opportunity.
2   An analysis of the nature of the problem.
3   An examination of alternative solutions, a weighting of these and a consideration of their likely consequences.
4   The implementation of the decision, including overcoming resistance.
5   A review and evaluation of the decision.

Building block 7: Appropriate leadership

Not all teams need leaders of a permanent nature, and many developed teams are able to change their leadership to suit the circumstances. But whether led or managed continually by the same person or by a variety of people we all have views about the way in which we should be managed. Successful managers the world over differ in what they regard as good management but what all agree on is that the team that is dissatisfied with the way in which it is led will operate below maximum effectiveness. We all know the manager who rules by fear, who gets results by shouting, ordering and threatening. Often this manager appears to get the required results but is unlikely to lead a team of committed people all giving their best. By contrast there is the weak and ineffectual manager, who may be a nice, friendly sort of person whom everyone likes on a personal level but who too often lacks the will or ability to face up to difficult issues. Observers have noticed repeatedly that the way people lead and manage others is a product of the attitudes and assumptions they have about them. Douglas McGregor developed a model which shows this quite clearly and some of the activities about leadership included in *50 Activities for Teambuilding* are based on the model. It is a simple and effective way of explaining some of the major issues about leadership.

He noticed that one set of managers displayed a set of assumptions about others which he called Theory X. They appeared to believe that people:

(a)   were fundamentally lazy and had to be pushed to work;
(b)   were basically sly and only interested in their own benefit;
(c)   responded best when disciplined and controlled;
(d)   took notice of punishment and worked better because of it;
(e)   were not really interested in their jobs or the welfare of the organization and only worked against their will.

Another set of managers displayed assumptions which were fundamentally different and which he called Theory Y. These managers appeared to believe that people:

(a)   were fundamentally willing to work providing the jobs were meaningful;
(b)   were basically honest;
(c)   took an active interest in the welfare of the groups to which they belonged;
(d)   responded best when given responsibility and freedom of action and manoeuvre;
(e)   valued honest praise and resented excessive punishment;
(f)   were very interested in the quality of their working lives as well as their personal lives.

He also noticed that those managers exhibiting the Theory Y assumptions consistenty obtained better results and that their departments had higher outputs, their people showed more creativity and innovation, they had fewer labour problems and lower labour turnover, they had less waste and were generally able to obtain better and more profitable results.

This all sounds very simple until we look around and see many thousands of managers who appear to practise the Theory X assumptions and yet are very successful. Often this is because their own personal ability can get them the results they desire without needing to get the best out of others. However, good teamwork gets the best out of all the members of the team and that demands management or leadership style which is both flexible and appropriate.

Another key for the leader to get the most out of himself or herself and the team is delegation. Delegation is not only a way of enabling a leader or manager to devote time to other issues, it is also real management development and a key to the confidence a leader really feels for his team. Where delegation does not happen it is a barrier to both increased results for the team and development for the manager and his subordinates. Often a low level of delegation results from lack of confidence in subordinates, lack of time to train and develop subordinates or fear of the results of delegation. There are countless examples of managers not coping because they have too much to do and yet they accuse those who surround them of being 'idle or unenthusiastic'. Delegation should enhance rather than threaten a manager's status and any manager who claims indispensability is usually not delegating. Many managers find that effective delegation is based on the following:

1 A simple analysis of areas of accountability and those which it is possible to delegate.
2 A consideration both of which team members could tackle the area and which would welcome it as a development opportunity.
3 A consideration of the training which would be necessary for delegation to take place.

Chosen team members should always be willing to take on the extra responsibilities and the leader must be prepared to give full authority and support. There are often risks in delegation but although improvement and development often demand risks they also bring high rewards. Finally, always remember to review the progress of the delegation and be prepared to take action if things go wrong.

In observing really successful team leaders, ten characteristics of success frequently stand out. The successful team leader:

(a) is authentic and true to himself or herself and his or her own beliefs;
(b) uses delegation as an aid to achievement and development;
(c) is clear about the standards he wishes to achieve;
(d) is willing and able to give and receive trust and loyalty;
(e) has the personal strength to maintain the integrity and position of the team;
(f) is receptive to people's hopes, needs and dignity;
(g) faces facts honestly and squarely;
(h) encourages personal and team development;
(i) establishes and maintains sound working procedures;
(j) tries to make work a happy and rewarding place.

Building block 8: Regular review

Good teams understand not only the team's character and its role in the organization, but they look at the way the team works, how it makes decisions, deals with conflicts, etc.

Reviewing allows the team to learn from experience and consciously to improve teamwork. There are numerous ways of reviewing and all of them are essentially concerned with team members receiving feedback about their performance as individuals or about the performance of the team as a whole. The three most widely used ways of reviewing are described below.

THE TEAM REVIEWING ITS OWN PERFORMANCE

There are many different approaches and aids to doing this and some are contained within this book. The skills which a team needs to carry out meaningful reviews are not easy to acquire because they depend upon the development of some of the other characteristics explained earlier. For instance, both openness and trust are needed in ample quantities if the exercise is to be realistic. These skills and the willingness to use them can be encouraged by stressing the really positive contribution which regular review can make. Review can often be carried out during and after the completion of a task and once the skills have been mastered it becomes a way of life for the team.

USING AN OBSERVER

The most popular method is usually called 'process review' and it involves someone sitting outside the group and quietly observing what happens. Often a prompt sheet itemizes the various points to be observed. This observer is really looking for the acts or words which helped the group in its task and those which did not, and at the end of the task, or at some convenient time during it, will present any observations for discussion. Care must be taken to report only what has been seen and not to colour the facts with opinions. The skills of really good process observations are again difficult to acquire but anyone who has mastered them can be a real help in the development of effective teams and of individuals.

CLOSED CIRCUIT TELEVISION

In the hands of someone who is both a skilled observer and a skilled operator of the equipment, CCTV can be a most powerful tool. The team can be recorded when it is performing a task and then the whole or part of the recording is played back. Whenever a team member requests it or whenever the operator thinks it appropriate the tape can be stopped and the team given the opportunity to analyse the incident just shown. All are able to see for themselves what actually happened and individuals are able to observe the effects on the team of their own interventions. In this way learning can be greatly speeded up and although equipment is expensive to purchase or to hire the savings in time and increases in learning usually more than justify its use.

Clearly, a CCTV set cannot be included with this manual nor can detailed guidance on its use be given here, but *50 Activities for Teambuilding* includes a variety of review instruments which can be used by team members or by observers. All of them have been effectively used many times to help teambuilding.

Regular review can improve team performance by:

(a)   ensuring that adequate effort is directed towards planning;
(b)   improving decision-making;
(c)   increasing support, trust, openness and honesty;
(d)   clarifying objectives;
(e)   identifying development needs and opportunities;
(f)   increasing the effectiveness of team leadership;

(g)   making meetings more productive and more enjoyable;
(h)   decreasing the number of emergencies and crises;
(i)   increasing involvement and commitment.

It is simply a question of learning how to function more effectively in the future by looking at the way the team is operating in the present.

Building block 9: Individual development

Effective teamwork seeks to pool the skills of individuals and to produce better results by so doing. Whilst the effectiveness of the team can be greater than the sum of the parts it also follows that effective teams need to pay attention to the development of individual skills. Just as different societies have different views of the developed group so throughout the history of man different societies and cultures have had different views as to what constitutes the developed and effective individual. As one obvious fact about teams is that they are a collection of individuals, then their effectiveness must in part be a function of individual ability.

Often when organizations look at personal development issues they are seen in terms of the skills and knowledge which individuals possess and training strategies are geared to improving them. But, of course, it is never as simple as that. Business life is full of countless examples of executives who seem to have all the right skills and all the knowledge, technical and otherwise, and yet still never seem to achieve worthwhile results. We also meet many executives, particularly owner-managers, who have had little training and on the surface appear deficient in the accepted managerial skills, and yet they have created immensely successful businesses and seem to have the knack of always succeeding. In practice, management is not simply a question of skills and textbook knowledge, it is about seeing opportunities, seizing them and making things happen, and some people seem able to do that continually. Observers have noticed that the most effective and the least effective almost invariably display two different sets of characteristics (see page 106). The less effective seem to have a passive approach to life wishing to be undisturbed as much as possible. They find challenge frightening and avoid it whenever possible. They also avoid insight into themselves and their beliefs. They do not welcome feedback from others and criticism, far from being healthy, is seen as unhelpful and threatening. They are not in touch with their own feelings, and do not wish to be, and new experiences are avoided because of the potential threat which they could bring. Often they try to manipulate others and seldom do they seek to increase the freedom of others. They lack concern for others and whilst they may give sympathy to them they rarely offer real help. Their beliefs are basically the beliefs of others, often learned in childhood and seldom seriously questioned; they are not authentic people. They are intolerant of the views of others and are often heard to bemoan the fact that others are not like them. In their unrelaxed posture towards life they are content with low standards for themselves and for others and when difficult problems arise they are the first to shun responsibility. For them life would be happier if they were surrounded by weak people but they are not and so often they resent the strong who they see contributing substantially to their basically unhappy and unsatisfactory lives.

Successful people by contrast seem to have an active approach to life. They are the people who make things happen and are constantly seeking new challenges for themselves and the groups which they represent. They wish to know more about themselves and are interested in the feedback which others can give them about both their strengths and their weaknesses. They welcome constructive criticism. They recognize that time and energy are limited in terms of human existence and, seeing them as man's most valuable resources, they plan their lives to make the most of them. They constantly seek new experiences because they see the quality of life being linked to the range of experience which an individual can encompass. By constantly achieving good results they build a reputation as people who can be relied upon to 'come up with the goods' and they are committed to seeing things through even when difficult situations arise. They understand their own feelings and try to use them as a positive force in their relationships with others. They care about others and their feelings and whilst they may not always agree they remain tolerant to the beliefs of those around them. They strive to be open with others, for they have nothing to hide and they realize that honesty is a much neglected value but is usually the best course. They are not frightened to give freedom to others, realizing that personal growth requires room to grow. They set high standards for themselves and the groups which they represent and are constantly seeking opportunities to extend themselves and their colleagues. Because they have worked things through for themselves they are clear about their own beliefs and are not inhibited by the teachings of others. Because they are successful they are strong and they rejoice in that strength using it as a positive force for themselves and their colleagues. They are relaxed, happy people who see life as an adventure which they enjoy immensely.

Usually, no-one displays totally either one or the other set of characteristics; it is a question of degree, and individual development is essentially about which set of characteristics we move towards and which we move away from. The two sets of characteristics when placed side by side become stark alternatives; choices which we are able to make about ourselves, our approach to life and our approach to work. Often those individuals who predominantly exhibit the high effectiveness characteristics are uncomfortable people to work with, their drive and dynamism at first sight appearing to inhibit the common good of the team. The really effective teams, however, learn to capitalize on these qualities and encourage their less effective members to move towards them.

SUMMARY OF HIGH/LOW EFFECTIVENESS CHARACTERISTICS

High effectiveness characteristics	Low effectiveness characteristics
1 Active	1 Passive
2 Seek challenge	2 Avoid challenge
3 Seek insight into themselves	3 Avoid self-knowledge
4 See and use time and energy as valuable resources	4 Misuse time and energy
5 In touch with their feelings	5 Out of touch with their feelings
6 Show concern for others	6 Do not care for others' feelings
7 Relaxed	7 Tense
8 Open and honest	8 Use manipulation
9 Stretch themselves	9 Avoid stretching experiences
10 Clear personal values	10 Programmed by the views of others
11 Set high standards	11 Set low standards
12 Welcome feedback	12 Avoid feedback
13 See things through	13 Opt out
14 Tolerate and use opposing views	14 Intolerant to others' views
15 Use conflict constructively	15 Avoid conflict
16 Give freedom	16 Restrain freedom
17 Are happy about life	17 Unhappy about life

Building block 10: Sound inter-group relations

No man is an island and rarely is a team. No matter how well a team exhibits

(a) balanced roles,
(b) clear objectives,
(c) openness and confrontation,
(d) support and trust,
(e) co-operation and conflict,
(f) sound procedures,
(g) appropriate leadership,
(h) regular review,
(i) individual development, and
(j) good communications

its success will be hindered if it lacks good relationships with other groups or individuals. The cohesive team can so often appear as a threat to other groups who perceive that they are less effective and this can so easily lead to cool relationships or hostility. Just as teamwork is individuals working well together so effective organizational life is partially teams relating to and performing well together. Thus, the really effective team is constantly reaching out to others to ensure that its efforts are well received and supported and to ensure that help from others will be forthcoming when needed.

Effective external relationships are:

1 Ensuring that the actions and decisions of the team are communicated and understood.

2   Recognizing that although teams are not the same that is no reason for them to stay apart.
3   Trying to understand the other team's point of view, recognizing their problems and difficulties and offering a hand of friendship when needed.
4   Continually seeking out ways of working effectively with others.
5   Not being too rigid in defending team boundaries.
6   Recognizing that boundaries and responsibilities between teams will need to be reviewed and amended from time to time.
7   Anticipating and eliminating potential inter-team problems before they arise.
8   Really trying to listen to others and doing all that is possible to help them listen to you.
9   Using others as a source of ideas and comparison.
10   Understanding and utilizing differences in people.

Once achieved, effective inter-group relationships bring a host of advantages. Amongst the foremost of these are greater ability to influence the organization, more available help, easier flow of information, easier problem solving, less anxiety and happier, more enjoyable working lives.

It follows that to have sound external relationships teams must exhibit and use many of the characteristics outlined earlier. Many of the building blocks of effective teamwork are also the bridges to other teams. Many teams have foundered because, although they were highly developed internally, they omitted to build those bridges which are so necessary to link the team with other parts of the organization.

Internal barriers can be overcome by:

- Bringing different teams and departments together physically to plan together and to ensure that differing roles and objectives are clarified and understood.
- Getting to know members of other teams, especially new members or those who have little opportunity to relate to people outside of their own working group.
- Developing informal structures and opportunities which enable people to be open with each other. Meetings, club and social events can be used.
- Setting up joint meetings where issues can be aired, where routine communications can be reviewed and where conflicts can be resolved.

- Arranging joint training. Often separate teams have shared learning needs and training programmes can provide an additional opportunity for breaking down barriers.
- Improving inter-group communications (see section on good communications – many of the principles apply).
- Developing Win–Win contracts. Just because teams want and need to win, it does not mean that others always have to lose!

Building block 11: Good communications

Communication is the oil for the machinery. Or to select another metaphor, it is the power train linking the engine to the drive wheels.

Probably the most heard complaint in any organization is that 'our communications are poor'. Ask any group of employees and you will almost invariably get the same answer, 'Our communications are in need of improvement'. This is not surprising if we consider the complexity of the pattern of communications in organizations. Effective communication is necessary at and between every level in an organization, between its constituent parts and with the many groups which comprise the external environment.

- Individuals have a need to communicate effectively.
- Teams have a need to communicate effectively.
- Organizations have a need to communicate effectively.

Each needs to communicate to some extent with the other and depending upon the role, most need to communicate with the external environment. Within an organization; as problems become more and more complex, there is an increasing need for complex solutions which utilize the abilities of greater numbers of people often cutting across traditional hierarchical relationships.

Where trades unions are influential in labour relations it is those organizations which can communicate effectively with them who are best placed to avoid industrial unrest.

It is those developments within an organization which are

communicated effectively with others that are likely to secure co-operation and thus their aims.

Within the market place, as competition becomes more and more fierce it is those organizations which can communicate with customers and suppliers who are likely to be most competitive.

Within cultures it is those organizations which can communicate effectively with governments that are most likely to influence government policy and legislation and hence their own competitive position.

It is those organizations that communicate best with universities, schools and colleges which, other things being equal, are likely to attract the best recruits.

In any programme of team development an examination of communications issues is an essential part.

COMMUNICATIONS WITHIN THE TEAM

The model overleaf indicates some of the many patterns of communications which can be reviewed within the team, with other units in the organization and with the external environment.

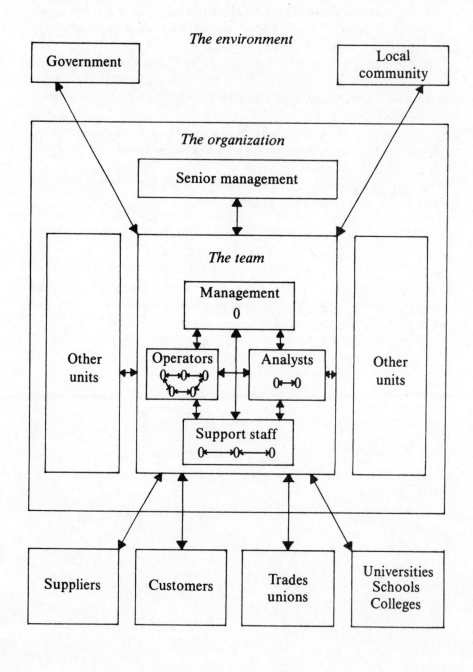

With the effective team, good communication is necessary between members with the same specialization and between different specializations. Within teams there will be:

- *Managers* who direct, control and co-ordinate.
- *Operators* who perform the central task.
- *Analysts* who innovate and rationalize.
- *Support staff* who enable the central task to be performed.

All need to communicate with the others both as individuals and sub-groups.

Communications within the team can be enhanced by

(a) improving the communications skills of individual team members
(b) facilitating a better flow of information and ideas.

THE SKILLED COMMUNICATOR

As we examine people who consistently communicate well we can identify the requirements of the skilled communicator.

First of all the communicator will have a well developed sense of how his or her views, attitudes and actions impact on others. Personal strengths and weaknesses will be known. In short, s/he will have self knowledge.

Sureness of beliefs and values and honesty in dealings with others are important. As Shakespeare wrote, 'To thine own self be true and it must surely follow as night follows day that thou cannot be false to any other man'.

An ability to deal with all types of people in differing situations, the capacity to be flexible in approach according to need are a mark of the communicator with interpersonal skills.

This person will be a good listener, actively listening and trying to 'hear' what others are really saying. As John Dunn said, 'There are those who listen and there are those who wait to talk'.

A manager, supervisor or a leader of a sub-group will have the ability to atune his leadership style to meet the needs of those being led, recognizing that different people and different tasks require differing approaches from those who lead. This is leadership flexibility.

A communicator is a person who is perceived by others as 'worth listening to'. People will take notice of views when a person is seen to stand up for beliefs and if necessary to fight for them. Opposition will not cow such a person whose assertiveness and presence will cope with any situation.

This person will recognize that often communication requires learning and that what is to be communicated to others may not be readily understandable by them. A willingness and ability to help others learn presuppose training and counselling skills.

This person will be able to communicate in the written word as well as face to face and will, therefore, require writing skills.

To stand up in front of a group and put a case over well and professionally will need presentation skills.

Because there may be a need to bring together people with differing viewpoints and contributions and utilize the whole of what they have to offer he or she will have to be a competent Chairman.

Overall, sensitivity to the needs, feelings and perceptions of others and an understanding of relationship requirements as well as task requirements is expected. The communicator will have sensitivity.

Some of these requirements are skills which can be learned through formal traning sessions. Others are personal attributes which, whilst training can help, are more difficult to acquire, being the product of the kind of person that we are. Development of these requirements is more a question of personal questioning and experiment.

Ten requirements of the skilled communicator

Personal attributes	Skills
Self knowledge	Interpersonal skills
Honesty	Listening skills
Sensitivity	Training and counselling skills
Flexibility	Writing skills
Assertiveness and presence	Chairmanship skills

FACILITATING BETTER COMMUNICATIONS

Often communications within a team can be improved by making relatively minor changes in working practices, but some improvements require more fundamental work with team members. The following are all actions which can be initiated or developed to improve communications.

1 *Attitude surveys*	These can throw new light on how team members are feeling and what the barriers to better communication are.
2 *Appraisal/counselling*	Either a formal or informal system can greatly improve willingness and ability to communicate.
3 *Mass communications*	Using works newspapers, notice boards, bulletins, books and manuals, etc. to get the message over.
4 *Cascading*	Using the differing levels of management to 'Cascade' information down and up the team.
5 *Getting to know others*	Often people can work together for years without really knowing their colleagues. Activities and training sessions can be used to develop and open up relationships.
6 *Works representatives*	Works Councils and other employee representative groups, even trades unions can be used to get the message across, although there are dangers in using agencies 'outside the team' to communicate information which is generated within the team.
7 *Systematic planning*	Often people are reluctant to be part of the action because they have not been part of the planning process which has gone before. Involvement at the planning stage encourages free communication at the action stage.
8 *Working environment*	Often the mere layout of desks or workstations inhibits free communication. Ask how necessary separate offices/workrooms really are and whether they are acting as a barrier to communications. Territorial barriers are barriers to communication.

9 *Eliminating unearned status symbols*	Seniority and status should be based on ability and contribution. Status symbols which are not perceived to be fully earned inhibit communication.
10 *Value clarification*	People will communicate better when they share a common perception of what the team stands for.

Rudyard Kipling wrote, 'I keep six honest serving men, they taught me all I know, their names are what and why and when and where and how and who'.

Good communication implies that these questions are regularly asked and answered openly and honestly.

The building blocks checklist

This simple checklist approach enables a team to undertake an on-the-spot review of performance after the completion of an everyday activity or task. It will also provide a checklist of improvement targets for future activities or tasks.

First ask each team member to complete the Review sheet answering each question Yes or No.

Then pool the answers to each question by adding up the Yes answers to arrive at a ranking for each of the eleven items. Record the results on the ranking sheet.

Next discuss the ranking which is thrown up by the pooled results. Spend five or ten minutes discussing each item and inviting those whose answer was in a minority to explain their reasons.

In the light of the insights gained re-rank with the items *as a team*. Use the re-ranking sheet to do this.

Now pick two or three of the weakest items and brainstorm ideas on how the team can improve performance. Develop a Checklist to use on further activities, use the Performance checklist sheet to record the conclusions.

The process can be repeated after other activities or tasks as often as the team feels that the exercise is valuable.

The companion volume *50 Activities for Teambuilding* contains other practical methods of using the building blocks approach to review and improve team performance.

Review sheet

1 Did we have the right mix of team members? Yes ☐ No ☐

2 Were we clear what we wanted to achieve? Yes ☐ No ☐

3 Were we sufficiently open and did we confront the real issues? Yes ☐ No ☐

4 Did we support and trust each other? Yes ☐ No ☐

5 Did we co-operate with each other and use the conflict of ideas and approaches productively? Yes ☐ No ☐

6 Were our working procedures and decision making strategies sound? Yes ☐ No ☐

7 Were we well led? Yes ☐ No ☐

8 Did we review whether we could operate in a better way? Yes ☐ No ☐

9 Did we utilize opportunities for development? Yes ☐ No ☐

10 Were our relations with other groups productive? Yes ☐ No ☐

11 Did we communicate well? Yes ☐ No ☐

Ranking sheet

Ranking

Item 1 Balanced roles

Item 2 Clear objectives and agreed goals

Item 3 Openness and confrontation

Item 4 Support and trust

Item 5 Co-operation and conflict

Item 6 Sound procedures

Item 7 Appropriate leadership

Item 8 Regular review

Item 9 Individual development

Item 10 Sound inter-group relations

Item 11 Good communications

Re-ranking sheet

Re-ranking

Item 1   Balanced roles

Item 2   Clear objective and agreed goals

Item 3   Openness and confrontation

Item 4   Support and trust

Item 5   Co-operation and conflict

Item 6   Sound procedures

Item 7   Appropriate leadership

Item 8   Regular review

Item 9   Individual development

Item 10   Sound inter-group relations

Item 11   Good communications

Performance checklist sheet

Item for Improvement
Checklist:

Item for Improvement
Checklist:

Item for Improvement
Checklist:

PART IV
SELECTING TEAMBUILDING ACTIVITIES

On the following pages you will find a guide to the collection of activities which have been assembled in the companion volume, *50 Activities for Teambuilding*. This guide indicates which activities can be used to help understand and bring about:

1   balanced roles;
2   clear objectives and agreed goals;
3   openness and confrontation;
4   support and trust;
5   co-operation and conflict;
6   sound procedures;
7   appropriate leadership;
8   regular review;
9   individual development;
10   sound inter-group relations;
11   good communications.

These of course are the eleven 'building blocks' of effective teamwork referred to earlier.

First the purpose of each activity is given with a list of the building blocks which it can aid.

Secondly a quick reference key is included which gives an at-a-glance link between the building blocks and the activities.

1   OUR TEAM AND ITS STAGE OF DEVELOPMENT

To provide a simple structural way in which team members can consider the performance and stage of development of their own teams.
Aids building blocks:

2   Clear objectives
3   Openness and confrontation
4   Support and trust
5   Co-operation and conflict
6   Sound procedures
7   Appropriate leadership
8   Regular review
9   Individual development
11   Good communications

2   WHAT MAKES TEAMS EFFECTIVE

To promote understanding of and agreement about 'the characteristics of effective teams'.
Aids building blocks:

6   Sound procedures
8   Regular review
9   Individual development

3   TEAM RATING

To compare teams by assessing them against the characteristics which are commonly associated with success, and to help identify those teams which may be most in need of development, and provide a basis for helping them.

Aids building blocks:

8   Regular review
9   Individual development
10   Sound inter-group relations

4   *THE TEAMS IN MY WORKING LIFE*

This activity helps to identify the various groups of teams to which we belong in our working lives and examines why some are more effective than others.

Aids building blocks:

9   Individual development
10   Sound inter-group relations

5   *TEAM MIRRORING*

To see ourselves and our team as others see us. All of us form views of other groups of people. Sometimes these views are accurate, but often they act as a barrier to working together effectively. This barrier can sometimes be removed if we understand what we think about others and know what they think about us.

Aids building blocks:

3   Openness and confrontation
4   Support and trust
8   Regular review
10   Sound inter-group relations
11   Good communications

6   *TEAM LEADER EFFECTIVENESS*

To enable team leaders to assess their own effectiveness as leaders by self-appraisal.

Aids building blocks:

7   Appropriate leadership
9   Individual development

7   *TEAM LEADERSHIP STYLE*

Almost more than anything else, the way in which a team is led can affect the contribution and performance of those who work in it. This activity enables a team and its leader(s) to examine their assumptions about people and about management style. Based on McGregor's Theory X and Y approach, it helps reveal what attitudes influence the team so that, brought into the open, these attitudes can be dealt with more effectively.
   Aids building blocks:

1   Balanced roles
7   Appropriate leadership
8   Regular review
9   Individual development
11   Good communications

8   *CHARACTERISTICS OF PERSONAL EFFECTIVENESS*

Developed and successful individuals the world over display a set of fairly common characteristics. In the same way others continually display a set of characteristics regularly associated with being less successful. This activity is designed to help you see where you stand in relation to the two lists.
   Aids building blocks:

1   Balanced roles
7   Appropriate leadership
8   Regular review
9   Individual development

9   *MY MEETINGS WITH OTHERS*

Almost all of us regularly meet others in our working lives and whether the meetings are formal or informal we can usually make

them more useful. This activity helps to assess our present effectiveness and move towards improvement.
    Aids building blocks:

  9   Individual development
10   Sound inter-group relations
11   Good communications

10   *FORCE FIELD ANALYSIS*

To provide a framework for a team to tackle a difficult problem systematically.
    Aids building blocks:

2   Clear objectives
6   Sound procedures
9   Individual development

11   *TEAM EFFECTIVENESS ACTION PLAN*

During a training event to enable participants to consider how team effectiveness can be increased 'back home'.
    Aids building blocks:

  2   Clear objectives
  6   Sound procedures
  8   Regular review
11   Good communications

12   *BRAINSTORMING*

Many normal operating rules in teams restrict creativity. This activity helps to generate creative ideas and shows how much easier it is to do that when the normal constraints are removed.
    Aids building blocks:

2   Clear objectives
3   Openness and confrontation

6   Sound procedures
9   Individual development

13   TEAM OPENNESS EXERCISE

Team effectiveness can be advanced by greater openness amongst team members. This activity helps team members to be more open with each other by exploring work-related topics in greater depth.
  Aids building block:

3   Openness and confrontation

14   REVIEW AND APPRAISAL MEETINGS

In any team there needs to be constant concern with 'what has to be done' and 'how best results can be achieved'. A discipline of regular target setting and review often helps team members to work more effectively. In addition, the intention is to give each employee an accurate view of how the company values his contribution and to enable all concerned to understand what has to be done in order to improve performance. Special attention is paid to what the person needs to learn in order to better meet future needs.
  Aids building blocks:

1   Balanced roles
6   Sound procedures
7   Appropriate leadership
11   Good communications

15   ENLIVENING MEETINGS

Often regular meetings become dull and uninteresting and people do not contribute at their optimum level. This activity is designed to increase the involvement of all participants in a regular meeting.
  Aids building blocks:

2   Clear objectives
6   Sound procedures

8   Regular review
11 Good communications

16 HOW GOOD A COACH ARE YOU?

To allow those who lead teams to assess their own attitude and practices towards developing others by means of coaching. The activity also gives valuable pointers to the skills and behaviour required of a good coach.
  Aids building blocks:

1   Balanced roles
7   Appropriate leadership
9   Individual development

17 BEING A BETTER COACH

The team leader has a vital role to play in the development of his team by operating as a coach or counsellor. Many team leaders accept this as sound common sense and have a genuine desire to play their part. For a variety of reasons – time or work pressures, disapproval from others, unwillingness to break new ground – this desire is often not converted into reality. Sometimes team leaders feel they have not got the expertise to master this new 'technique'.
  Aids building blocks:

7   Appropriate leadership
9   Individual development

18 COUNSELLING TO INCREASE LEARNING

This activity enables two colleagues to assist each other in defining and tackling their individual developments needs.
  Aids building blocks:

7   Appropriate leadership
9   Individual development

19 MANAGEMENT STYLE

To enable participants to examine their own beliefs about people against McGregor's Theory X-Y model. To provide direct feedback of how others perceive a person's management style. To stimulate general discussion about management style.
    Aids building blocks:

3   Openness and confrontation
4   Support and trust
5   Co-operation and conflict
7   Appropriate leadership
9   Individual development

20 DISCUSSING VALUES

To facilitate discussion of 'value issues' which are commonly found in working teams. Often people are accustomed to discussing facts but less used to discussing issues which involve values, feelings and emotions.
    Aids building blocks:

3   Openness and confrontation
4   Support and trust
5   Co-operation and conflict

21 TEAM MEMBER DEVELOPMENT NEEDS

In the end people must be responsible for their own development. Organizations can create learning opportunities but only individuals can utilize them. If team members are to feel responsibility for, and ownership of, their own development, they need to be involved in establishing their own development needs and they need to take steps to aid their own development. This activity is designed to help individual team members to do this.
    Aids building block:

9   Individual development

22 WHO ARE YOU?

To develop relationships as a prelude to working on deeper issues. To practise listening skills.
  Aids building blocks:

  3   Openness and confrontation
  9   Individual development
  10 Sound inter-group relations
  11 Good communications

23 INTIMACY EXERCISE

Most working relationships exist at a fairly superficial level. This activity is designed to help us get to know others in greater depth. Its specific aims are:

  (a) to experience self-disclosure;
  (b) to accelerate the getting-acquainted process in teams;
  (c) to experience talking about taboo topics;
  (d) to develop authenticity between team members.
    Aids building blocks:

  3   Openness and confrontation
  4   Support and trust
  10 Sound inter-group relations

24 HIGHWAY CODE – A CONSENSUS-SEEKING ACTIVITY

  1 To study information-sharing and consensus-seeking activity within a group.
  2 To contrast the results of individual and group decision-making.
  3 To study the features of effective group working.
    Aids building blocks:

  2 Clear objectives
  5 Co-operation and conflict
  6 Sound procedures

7   Appropriate leadership
10 Sound inter-group relations

25   *IS THE TEAM LISTENING?*

'There are those who listen and those who wait to talk'. Many of the activities associated with helping groups to develop require a high level of listening skill. Some people are naturally good at this while others are poor. Some people find it difficult to accept the importance of listening. This activity helps develop this skill in teams. It can prove a rewarding, revealing and, on occasions, amusing activity.

   Aids building blocks:

4   Support and trust
6   Sound procedures
9   Individual development
11 Good communications

26   *CAVE RESCUE*

To study 'values' in group decision making. To practise consensus seeking behaviour.

   Aids building blocks:

3   Openness and confrontation
5   Co-operation and conflict
6   Sound procedures
10 Sound inter-group relations

27   *INITIAL REVIEW*

This activity is designed to provide information about how team members view the team to which they belong as a prelude to further action.

   Aids building blocks:

8   Regular review

28   *PRISONER'S DILEMMA*

Often we are more concerned with winning than with achieving the optimum result. This well-tested activity is designed for the following purposes:

1   To explore the trust between team members and the effect of trust betrayal on team members.
2   To demonstrate the effects of competition between teams.
3   To demonstrate the potential advantages of a collaborative approach to solving problems.
4   To demonstrate the necessity of establishing the purpose of any activity.
    Aids building blocks:

2   Clear objectives
3   Openness and confrontation
4   Support and trust
5   Co-operation and conflict
7   Appropriate leadership
10   Sound inter-group relations

29   *THE ZIN OBELISK*

1   To study the process of information sharing in teams.
2   To study leadership, co-operation and conflict issues.
    Aids building blocks:

2   Clear objectives
3   Openness and confrontation
5   Co-operation and conflict
6   Sound procedures
7   Appropriate leadership
10   Sound inter-group relations

30   *CLOVER LEAF*

To provide an opportunity for teams to study use of resources and creativity. Any number of teams with a minimum of six players each may take part.

Aids building blocks:

2 Clear objectives
6 Sound procedures
7 Appropriate leadership
8 Regular review
10 Sound inter-group relations

31 FOUR-LETTER WORDS

To provide an opportunity for a team to study a range of teamwork issues whilst performing a task which makes increasing demands on them.

Aids building blocks:

2 Clear objectives
6 Sound procedures
8 Regular review
10 Sound inter-group relations

32 TEAM TASKS

To provide ideas for simple tasks which a team can complete in a short time and which will provide a basis for reviewing and learning from performance.

Aids building blocks:

2 Clear objectives
3 Openness and confrontation
4 Support and trust
5 Co-operation and conflict
6 Sound procedures
7 Appropriate leadership
8 Regular review
10 Sound inter-group relations

33   *MAKING MEETINGS MORE CONSTRUCTIVE*

Meeting are probably regarded as the major curse of modern organizational life. It is not that meetings are a bad thing, it is just that so many are badly used. This activity aims to show that they can be improved and made more constructive if the following features are present:

(a)   clear purpose and objectives;
(b)   maximum involvement of all participants;
(c)   clear and agreed procedures;
(d)   review of 'what is going on in the meeting' (the process at regular intervals.

Aids building blocks:

2   Clear objectives
3   Openness and confrontation
6   Sound procedures
7   Appropriate leadership
8   Regular review
10   Sound inter-group relations

34   *POSITIVE AND NEGATIVE FEEDBACK*

Personal feedback is a feature of many teambuilding events and activities. Often the negative feedback can appear as extremely threatening and can lead to feelings of insecurity. This can be lessened by ensuring that it is accompanied by positive feedback which enhances a feeling of well-being and security. This activity is designed to facilitate both negative and positive feedback simultaneously.

Aids building blocks:

3   Openness and confrontation
4   Support and trust
10   Sound inter-group relations
11   Good communications

35 IMPROVING ONE-TO-ONE RELATIONSHIPS

Sometimes two people who need to work together seem to be constantly at loggerheads. We may feel inclined to knock their heads together. This sometimes works but it is not a development technique which can always be recommended as often the result is nothing better than severe headaches! This activity aims to bring about improvement by:

(a) specifying what each expects of the other;
(b) clarifying where those expectations are not being met;
(c) clarifying how the two can be more helpful to each other.
      Aids building blocks:

3 Openness and confrontation
4 Support and trust
5 Co-operation and conflict
9 Individual development
10 Sound inter-group relations

36 TO SEE OURSELVES AS OTHERS SEE US

To experience and demonstrate openness as a feature of a teambuilding event. To generate further data for use at the event.
      Aids building blocks:

3 Openness and confrontation
4 Support and trust
8 Regular review
10 Sound inter-group relations

37 PROCESS REVIEW

Process review is one way of studying meetings or activities for the purpose of improving teamwork. Teams become effective by looking at the way they function and by learning from experience.
      Aids building blocks:

1   Balanced roles
8   Regular review

38   *HOW WE MAKE DECISIONS*

This activity is designed to help participants determine their predominant decision-making style by receiving feedback from other people, and to help a team to establish the decision-making style most frequently used.
Aids building blocks:

4   Support and trust
6   Sound procedures
8   Regular review

39   *TEAM SELF-REVIEW*

To help team effectiveness by reviewing performance. Whilst process review involves the use of an 'outsider' internal review can be conducted without such help.
Aids building blocks:

1   Balanced roles
8   Regular review

40   *SILENT SHAPES*

To study problem solving and communication techniques within a team in order to apply the learning in a work situation.
Aids building blocks:

4   Support and trust
6   Sound procedures
11   Good communications

41 BASIC MEETING ARRANGEMENTS

Often regular meetings follow a set format which inhibits contribution and effectiveness. This activity is designed to highlight which of the 'basics' of meetings need improvement. The activity deals with the 'basics' of meetings rather than interpersonal issues.

Aids building blocks:

2 Clear objectives
6 Sound procedures
7 Appropriate leadership

42 DECISION-TAKING

To enable a team leader to examine how his team members perceive decisions to be taken, and to contrast this with how they would wish decisions to be taken.

Aids building blocks:

6 Sound procedures
7 Appropriate leadership
8 Regular review

43 COMMUNICATION SKILLS INVENTORY

To provide a structure for reviewing personal communication skills. To enable a communication skills improvement plan to be formulated.

Aids building blocks:

1   Balanced roles
9   Individual development
11 Good communications

44 TEAM STOCK-TAKE

The first step in the team development process is to visualize where the team is now. Later it is important to keep checking on the

progress made and to establish a common perception of how far the team has travelled and where it is now.
   Aids building blocks:

8   Regular review
11 Good communications

45   MY ROLE IN THE TEAM

To enable individual team members to consider the roles which they play within the team and identify which roles could be developed and used more to increase their effectiveness.
   Aids building blocks:

1   Balanced roles
7   Appropriate leadership
9   Individual development
11 Good communications

46   DEVISING A TEAM VISION

To enable a team to develop a vision of its future organisation and to review how it communicates its vision to the rest of the organization.
   Aids building blocks:

1   Balanced roles
2   Clear objectives
6   Sound procedures
11 Good communications

47   INTER-GROUP FEEDBACK

To develop open communication with other teams in the organization.
   Aids building blocks:

2   Clear objectives
3   Openness and confrontation

8   Regular review
10 Sound inter-group relations
11 Good communications

48 BURYING THE OLD TEAM

Where teams have undergone rapid change which has involved a large proportion of new members joining, it is common to find that 'old' and 'new' camps emerge. This activity is designed to help bring together these different camps and create a more unified team.
   Aids building blocks:

2   Clear objectives
3   Openness and confrontation
4   Support and trust
7   Appropriate leadership
11 Good communications

49 ORGANIZATIONAL TYPES AUDIT

To provide an understanding of organizational types. To review communication requirements in different types of organization. To clarify what aspects of organizational communication require attention.
   Aids building block:

11 Good communications

50 BALANCING TEAM ROLES

One of the great strengths of effective teams lies in their blend of different talents and abilities. This activity enables a team to review its own blend of roles and to identify areas for improvement.
   Aids building blocks:

1   Balanced roles
7   Appropriate leadership
8   Regular review

Quick Reference Key Activities	Balanced roles	Clear objectives	Openness and confrontation	Support and trust	Co-operation and conflict	Sound procedures	Appropriate leadership	Regular review	Individual development	Sound inter-group relations	Good communications
1 Our team and its stage of development		*	*	*	*	*	*	*	*		*
2 What makes teams effective							*		*	*	
3 Team rating									*	*	
4 The teams in my working life									*	*	
5 Team mirroring			*	*					*	*	*
6 Team leader effectiveness							*		*		
7 Team leadership style	*						*	*	*		*
8 Characteristics of personal effectiveness	*						*	*	*		
9 My meetings with others									*	*	*
10 Force field analysis		*				*			*		
11 Team effectiveness action plan		*					*	*			*
12 Brainstorming		*	*			*			*		
13 Team openness exercise			*								
14 Review and appraisal meetings		*				*	*				*
15 Enlivening meetings		*				*		*			
16 How good a coach are you?		*					*		*		
17 Being a better coach							*		*		
18 Counselling to increase learning							*		*		
19 Management style			*	*	*		*		*		
20 Discussing values			*	*	*						
21 Team member development needs									*		
22 Who are you?			*						*	*	*
23 Intimacy exercise			*	*						*	
24 Highway code	*				*	*	*			*	
25 Is the team listening?				*		*				*	*
26 Cave rescue			*		*	*				*	
27 Initial review								*			
28 Prisoner's dilemma	*	*	*	*	*		*			*	

Quick Reference Key
concluded

Activities	Balanced roles	Clear objectives	Openness and confrontation	Support and trust	Co-operation and conflict	Sound procedures	Appropriate leadership	Regular review	Individual development	Sound inter-group relations	Good communications
29 The Zin obelisk		*	*		*	*	*			*	
30 Clover leaf		*				*	*	*		*	
31 Four letter words		*				*		*		*	
32 Team tasks		*	*	*	*	*	*	*		*	
33 Making meetings more constructive		*	*				*	*	*	*	
34 Positive and negative feedback			*	*						*	*
35 Improving one-to-one relationships			*	*	*				*	*	
36 To see ourselves as others see us			*	*				*		*	
37 Process review	*							*			
38 How we make decisions			*		*		*				
39 Team self-review	*							*			
40 Silent shapes				*		*					*
41 Basic meeting arrangements		*				*	*				
42 Decision-taking						*	*	*			
43 Communication skills inventory	*								*		*
44 Team stock-take								*			*
45 My role in the team	*						*		*		*
46 Devising a team vision	*	*					*				*
47 Intergroup feedback	*	*						*		*	*
48 Burying the old team	*	*	*					*			*
49 Organizational types audit											*
50 Balancing team roles	*						*	*	*		*

PART V
SOURCES OF FURTHER HELP

1   Publishers of management books

(a) UK

The following are publishers of management books. Lists of titles can be obtained from each.

W H Allen & Co plc
44 Hill Street
London
W1X 8LB

Basil Blackwell Publisher Ltd
108 Cowley Road
Oxford OX4 1JF

Century Hutchinson Publishing
   Group
Brookmount House
62–65 Chandos Place
London
WC2N 4NW

Collins Publishers
8 Grafton Street
London
W1X 3LA

Gower Publishing Company Ltd
Gower House
Croft Road
Aldershot
GU11 3HR

William Heinemann Ltd
Halley Court
Jordan Hill
Oxford
OX2 8EJ

Institute of Personnel
   Management
IPM House
Camp Road
Wimbledon
London
SW19 4UW

Kogan Page Ltd
120 Pentonville Road
London
N1 9JN

Longman Group Ltd
Longman House
Burnt Mill
Harlow
Essex
CM20 2JE

McGraw-Hill Book Co (UK) Ltd
McGraw-Hill House
Shoppenhangars Road
Maidenhead
Berks
SL6 2QL

MCB University Press Ltd
62 Toller Lane
Bradford
West Yorks
BD8 9BY

University Associates
  International Ltd
Challenge House
45–47 Victoria Street
Mansfield
Notts
NG18 5SU

John Wiley & Sons Ltd
Baffins Lane
Chichester
West Sussex
PO19 1UD

(b) USA

ACA Books
1285 Avenue of Americas
3rd fl Area M
New York
NY 10019

AMACOM Book Division
135 West 50th Street
New York
NY 10020–1201

American Arbitration
Association
140 W 51 St
New York
NY 10020–1203

American Hospital Publishing
  Inc
211 E Chicago Avenue
Chicago
IL 60611

American Sciences Press Inc
20 Cross Road
Syracuse
NY 13224–2144

Asher-Gallant Press
201 Montrose Road
Westbury
NY 11590

Aspen Publishers Inc
1600 Research Blvd
Rockville
MD 20850

Association of University
  Programs in Health
  Administration (AUPHA)
1191 N Fort Meyer Dr
Suite 503
Arlington
VA 22209

Atcom Inc Publishers
2315 Broadway,
New York
NY 10024

Auerback Publishers Inc
One Penn Plaza
New York
NY 10119

Battelle Press
505 King Avenue
Colombus
OH 43201-2693

Bell Publishing
15 Surrey Lane East Brunswick
NJ 08816

BNA Books
1231 St NW
Washington
DC 2037

Bonus Books Inc
160 E Illinois St
Chicago
IL 60611

Branden Press Inc
Box 843
17 Station St
Brookline Village
Boston
MA 02147

Bridge Publications Inc
1414 N Catalina St
Los Angeles,
CA 90027

Business & Legal Reports
64 Wall Street
Madison
CT 06443

Business Books Marketing
  Group
Box 6870-51 Torrance
CA 90504

Chatham House Publishers Inc
Box One
Chatham
NJ 07928

Chilton Book Co
Chilton Way
Radnor
PA 19089

The Conference Board Inc
845 Third Avenue
New York
NY 10022

Consultants News
Templeton Road
Fitzwilliam
NH 03447

The Corinthian Press
3592 Lee Road
Shaker Heights
OH 44120

Crain Books/NTC Business
  Books
4255 W Touhy Avenue
Lincolnwood
IL 60646

Crisp Publications Inc
95 First Street
Los Altos
CA 94022

Dame Publications Inc
7800 Bissonnet,
Suite 415 Houston
TX 77074

The Dartnell Corp
4660 Ravenswood Ave
Chicago
IL 60640

Dorset House Publishing Co Inc
353 W 12 St
New York
NY 10014

Executive Enterprises
  Publications Co Inc
22 W 21 St
New York
NY 10010–6904

Fairchild Books & Visuals
7 E 12 St
New York
NY 10003

The Fairmont Press Inc
700 Indian Trial
Lilburn
GA 30247

Folio Publishing Corp
Box 4949
6 River Bend
Stamford
CT 06840

Gulf Publishing Co
Book Division
Box 2608
Houston
TX 77252

Harvard Business School Press
Morgan 41
Boston
MA 02163

Health Administration Press
1021 E Huron St
Ann Arbor
MI 48104

Hive Publishing Co
Box 1004
Alpha Building
Easton
PA 18042

Human Resource Development
  Press
22 Amherst Rd
Amherst
MA 01002

The ICC Publishing Corp Inc
156 Fifth Ave
Suite 820
New York
NY 10010

IEE Press
345 E 47 St
New York
NY 10017

ILR Press
Cornell University
Div of New York State School of
Industrial & Labour Relations
Ithaca
NY 14851–0952

JAI Press Inc
Box 1678
55 Old Post Road
Suite 2
Greenwich
CT 06836

Jossey-Bass Inc Publishers
433 California St
San Francisco
CA 94104

B Klein Publications
Box 8503
Coral Springs
FL 33065

Kumarian Press Inc
630 Oakwood Ave
Suite 119,
West Hartford
CT 06110

David S Lake Publishers
19 Davis Dr
Belmont
CA 94002

Learning Resources Network
  (LERN)
Box 1448
Manhattan
KS 66502

Lomond Publications Inc
Box 88
Mount Airy
MD 21771

Longman Financial Services
  Institute
520 N Dearborn
Chicago
IL 60610

McCutchan Publishing Corp
2940 San Pablo Ave
Berkeley
CA 94702

Management Resources Inc
96 Morton St
New York
NY 10014

Master Media Ltd
301 W 52 St
3rd Fl
New York
NY 10019

Medical Economic Books
680 Kinderkamack Rd
Oradell
NJ 07649

Nichols Publishing Co
PO Box 96
New York
NY 10024

Oliver Wright Ltd Publications
  Inc
5 Oliver Wright Dr
Essex Junction
VT 05452

Omni Learning Institute
860 Merrimon Ave
Suite 320
Asheville
NC 28804

Petrocelli Books Inc
251 Wall St
Research Park
Princeton
NJ 08540

Practice Management Associates
  Ltd
10 Midland Ave
Newton
MA 02158

Probus Publishing Co
118 N Clinton Street
Chicago
IL 60606

Productivity Press Inc
Box 814
Cambridge
MA 02238

Ronin Publishing Inc
Box 1035
Berkeley
CA 94701

Roxbury Publishing Co
Box 491044
Los Angeles
CA 90049

Sage Publications Inc
2111 W Hillcrest Dr
Newbury Park
CA 91320

Special Libraries Association
  (SLA)
1700 18 St N W
Washington
DC 20009

Syntony Publishing
1450 Byron St
Palo Alta
CA 94301

The Taft Group
5130 MacArthur Blvd NW
Washington
DC 20016

Theatre Communications Group
355 Lexington Ave
New York
NY 10017

Thompson & Co Inc
4600 Longfellow Ave
Minneapolis
MN 55407-3638

University Associates Inc
8517 Production Avenue
San Diego
California 92121

The Urban Institute Press
2100 'M' St NW
Washington
DC 20037

Van Nostrand Reinhold Co Inc
115 Fifth Ave
New York
NY 10003

Whatever Publishing Inc
58 Paul Dr
San Rafael
CA 94903

Markus Wiener Publishing Inc
2901 Broadway
Suite 107
New York
NY 10025

Williamson Publishing Co
Church Hill Road
Charlotte
VT 05445

2 Selected management training organizations in the UK

Aldwark Management Training
  Ltd
106 Micklegate
York
YO1 1JX   Tel: 0904 647728

Ashridge Management College
Berkhamsted
Hertfordshire
HP4 1NS   Tel: 044 284 3491

BACIE (British Association for
  Commercial and Industrial
  Education)
16 Park Crescent
London
W1N 4AP   Tel: 01-636 5351

BIS Applied Systems Ltd
20 Upper Ground
London
SE1 9PN   Tel: 01-633 0866

Barleythorpe Management
  Centre
Barleythorpe
Oakham
Leicestershire
LE15 7ED   Tel: 0572 3711

The Bradford Management
  Centre
Heaton Mount
Keighley Road
Bradford
West Yorkshire
BD9 4JU   Tel: 0274 42299

Brathay Hall Trust
Brathay Hall
Ambleside
Cumbria
LA22 0HP   Tel: 05394 33041

British Institute of Management
Management House
Cottingham Road
Corby
Northants
NN17 1TT: Tel: 0536 204222

Brunel University
Uxbridge
Middlesex
UB8 3PH   Tel: 0895 56461
ext 215

C.M.T.C.–Management Training
  Centre
Woodland Grange
Leamington Spa
CV32 6RN   Tel: 0926 36621/5

The City University Business
  School
Management Development
  Centre
Frobisher Crescent
Barbican Centre
London
EC2 8HB   Tel: 01-910 0111

The College of Management
Dunchurch
Rugby
Warwickshire
CV22 6QW   Tel: 0788 810656

Cranfield School of
  Management
Cranfield
Bedford
MK43 0AL   Tel: 0234 751122

Fielden House Productivity
  Centre Ltd
856 Wilmslow Road
Didsbury
Manchester
M20 8RY   Tel: 061-445 2426

Guardian Business Services
119 Farringdon Road
London
EC1R 3DA   Tel: 01-278 6787

Henley, The Management
  College
Greenlands
Henley-on-Thames
Oxon
RG9 3AU   Tel: 0491 571454

Hoskyns Group Ltd
Hoskyns House
130 Shaftesbury Avenue
London
W1V 7DN   Tel: 01-434 2171

Industrial Society
Peter Runge House
3 Carlton House Terrace
London
SW1Y 5DG   Tel: 01-839 4300

Institute of Directors
116 Pall Mall
London
SW1Y 5ED   Tel: 01-839 1233

Institute of Manpower Studies
University of Sussex
Mantell Building
Falmer
Brighton
BN1 9RF   Tel: 0273 686751

Institute of Personnel
  Management
IPM House
Camp Road
Wimbledon
London
SW19 4UW   Tel: 01-946 9100

The Leadership Trust
Weston-Under-Penyard
Ross-on-Wye
Herefordshire
HR9 7YH   Tel: 0989 67667

London Graduate School of
  Business Studies
Sussex Place
Regent's Park
London
NW1 4SA   Tel: 01-262 5050

London Chamber of Commerce
  and Industry
69 Cannon Street
London
EC4N 5AB   Tel: 01-248 4444

Manchester Business School
Booth Street West
Manchester
M15 6PB   Tel: 061-273 8228

The Open University
Walton Hall
Milton Keynes
MK7 6AA   Tel: 0908 74066

O.T.M.A. Ltd
Victoria House
Southampton Row
London
WC1B 4DH   Tel: 01-405 4730

Pera Training
Nottingham Road
Melton Mowbray
Leicestershire
LE13 0PB   Tel: 0664 501264

Reed International plc
Training and Development
  Department
College House
Aylesford
Maidstone
Kent
ME20 7PR   Tel: 0622 77777
ext. 4285

Richmond Consultants Limited
20 The Ridgeway
Mount Arraratt Road
Richmond
Surrey
Tel: 01-948 0270

Roffey Park Management
  College
Forest Road
Horsham
West Sussex
RH12 4TD   Tel: 029383 644

St Helens School of
  Management Studies
Water Street
St Helens
Merseyside
WA10 1PZ   Tel: 0744 33766

Structured Training Limited
Concorde House
24 Warwick New Road
Royal Leamington Spa
CV32 5JH   Tel: 0926 37621/6

Sundridge Park Management
  Centre
Bromley
Kent
BR1 3TP   Tel: 01-460 8585

Tack Training International
Tack House
Longmore Street
London
SW1V 1JJ   Tel: 01-834 5001

Templeton College
The Oxford Centre for
  Management Studies
Kennington
Oxford
OX1 5NY   Tel: 0865 735422

Urwick Management Centre
Baylis House
Stoke Poges Lane
Slough
Berkshire
SL1 3PF   Tel: 0753 34111

West of England Management
  Centre
Engineers' House
The Promenade
Clifton Down
Bristol
BS8 3NB   Tel: 0272 731471

3 Suppliers of management films and videos in the UK

BBC Enterprises Ltd
Woodlands
Wood Lane
W12 0TT   Tel: 01-743 5588
ext. 2232

CFL Vision,
Chalfont Grove
Gerrards Cross
Bucks
SL9 8TN   Tel: 02407 4433

Gower Publishing Co Ltd
Gower House
Croft Road
Aldershot
Hampshire
GU11 3HR   Tel: 0252 331551

Guild Sound and Vision
6 Royce Road
Peterborough
PE1 5YB   Tel: 0733 315315

Industrial Society
Peter Runge House
3 Carlton House Terrace
London
SW1Y 5DG   Tel: 01-839 4300

Melrose Film Productions
8–12 Old Queen Street
London
SW1 9HP   Tel: 01-222 1744

Millbank Films Ltd
1 Adam Street
London
WC2N 6AW
Tel: 01-839 7176

Rank Training
PO Box 70
Great West Road
Brentford
Middlesex
TW8 9HR   Tel: 01-568 9222

University Associates
  International Limited
45–47 Victoria Street
Mansfield
Notts
NG18 5SU   Tel: 0623 640203

Video Arts
Dumbarton House
68 Oxford Street
London
W1N 9LA   Tel: 01-580 0652

4 Management consultants in the UK

The two professional organizations for management consultancy are:

The Management Consultants Association
11 West Halkin Street, London SW1W 8JL   Tel: 01-235 3897
and
The Institute of Management Consultants
32–33 Hatton Garden, London EC1W 8DL   Tel: 01-242 2140

The Management Consultancy Information Service maintains files on management consultants in the UK and use of the service is free. Address: 38 Blenheim Avenue, Gants Hill, Ilford, Essex IG2 6JQ Tel: 01 554 4695.

5 Industrial training boards in the UK

Industrial training boards are established under the provisions of the Industrial Training Acts 1964 and 1982 for the purpose of making provision for the training of persons over compulsory school age for employment in industry and commerce. The Industrial Training Boards are constituted for Great Britain. Northern Ireland has its own system of training boards, established under the Industrial Training Act (Northern Ireland) 1964.

Under the Acts, the Secretary of State for Employment has power to establish Industrial Trainng Boards by making industrial training orders, though he may not do so until he has consulted representative associations of employers and employees in the field concerned. Such consultations are carried out on his behalf by the Manpower Services Commission.

Some have done valuable work in the area of teambuilding and can offer relevant publications, training events and advice but discretion needs to be exercised by the user. In particular, it is worth bearing in mind that:

1 Boards do not all have the same views about development needs in their industries.
2 Some boards have done little work in the team development area and do not have real expertise to offer.
3 The skill and experience of the adviser is all-important so do not be afraid to challenge and question his or her views and the advice given. An adviser will respect you for it, otherwise you are probably better off without the advice.

Some boards also offer an information service and will lend out useful publications.

The following is a complete list of Industrial Training Boards:

Agricultural ITB
Bourne House
32–34 Beckenham Road
Beckenham
Kent
BR3 4PB
(Dir., D. C. Newman)

Clothing and Allied Products ITB
Tower House
Merrion Way
Leeds
LS2 8NY
(Chief Exec., J. W. Dearden)

Construction ITB
Dewhurst House
24 West Smithfield
EC1A 9JA
(Sec., J. A. Reynolds, OBE)

Engineering ITB
PO Box 176
54 Clarendon Road
Watford
Herts
WD1 1LB
(Sec., E. P. Jones)

Hotel and Catering ITB
International House
High Street
Ealing
W5 5DB
(Sec., W. A. Heaney)

Local Government Training Board
Arndale House
Arndale Centre
Luton
Beds
LU1 2TS
(Dir., M. G. Clarke)

Man-Made Fibres Industry Training Advisory Board
Gable House
40 High Street
Rickmansworth
Herts
WD3 1ER
(Gen. Manager, D. W. Ashby)

Offshore Petroleum
Offshore Training Centre
Forties Road
Montrose
Angus
DD10 9ET
(Sec., P. J. Bing, OBE)

Plastic Processing
Coppice House
Halesfield 7
Telford
Shropshire
TF7 4NA
(Chief Exec., J. C. Shearman)

6 Management organizations around the world

Because of the wide differences in role and the services offered it is difficult to categorize management organizations. However, for each of the principal countries of the world, the name and address of one or more organizations concerned with the development of management skills is given. These organizations will in most cases be in a position to direct enquirers to other organizations within that country who can offer more specific help with team building

The list is subdivided into:

1 The United Kingdom
2 The United States
3 The Rest of the World

1 THE UNITED KINGDOM

Association for Management
  Education and Development
Premier House
77 Oxford Street
London
W1R 1RB

Association of Business
  Executives
3 Station Parade
Balham High Road
London
SW12 9AZ

Association of Business
  Managers and Administrators
23 Sunnybank Road
Manchester
M13 0XF

Association of Management
  Consulting Organizations
Confederation House
Kildare Street
Dublin 2

British Institute of Management
Management House
Cottingham Road
Corby
Northamptonshire

Confederation of British
  Industry
Centre Point
103 Oxford Street
London
WC1A 1DU

Foundation for Management
  Education
Sun Alliance House
New Inn Hall Street
Oxford
OX1 2QE

Industrial Society
Peter Runge House
3 Carlton House Terrace
London
SW1 5D9

Institute of Administrative
  Management
40 Chatsworth Parade
Petts Wood
Orpington
Kent
PR5 1RW

Institute of Directors
116 Pall Mall
London
SW17 5ED

Institute of Management
  Consultants
32–33 West Halkin Street
London
SW1X 8JL

Institute of Management
  Services
1 Cecil Court
London Road
Enfield
Middlesex
EN2 6DD

Institute of Management
  Specialists
14 Hamilton Terrace
Royal Leamington Spa
Warwickshire
CV32 4LZ

Institute of Manpower Studies
University of Sussex
Mantell Building
Falmer
Brighton
BN1 9RF

Institute of Personnel
  Management
IPM House
Camp Road
Wimbledon
London
SW19 4UW

Institute of Production Engineers
66 Little Ealing Lane
London
W5 4XX

Local Authorities Management
  Services and Computer
  Committee
3 Buckingham Gate
London
SW1E 6JH

Management Association of SE
  Scotland
3 Randolph Crescent
Edinburgh
EH3 7UD

Management Buy-out
  Association
c/o Melville Technologies Ltd
Spring Road
Letchworth
Herts

Management Consultants
  Association
11 West Halkin Street
London
SW1X 8JL

MBO Society
Underriver Farm
Underriver
Sevenoaks
Kent
TN15 0SJ

Society for Long Range
  Planning
15 Belgrave Square
London
SW1X 8PU

2   THE UNITED STATES OF AMERICA

Administrative Management
  Society
Willow Grove
Pennsylvania
PA 19090

American Assembly of Collegiate
  Schools of Business
605 Ballas Road
Suite 220
St Louis
Missouri 63141

American Association of
  Industrial Management
2500 Office Centre
Maryland Road
Willow Grove
Pennsylvania
PA 19090

American Management
  Associations
135 West 50 Street
New York
NY 10020

American Society for Training &
  Development
1630 Duke Street
No 13332
Alexandria
VA 22314

Association of Systems
  Management
24587 Bagley Road
Cleveland
Ohio
OH 44138

Institute of Management
  Sciences
146 Westminster Street
Providence
Rhode Island
RI 02903

Institute of Public
  Administration
55 West 44th Street
New York
NY 10036

The Conference Board
845 Third Avenue
New York
NY 10022

The Council for International
  Progress in Management (US)
  Inc (CIPM)
845 Third Avenue
New York

3 THE REST OF THE WORLD

International

European Council of
  Management (CECIOS)
Secretary c/o RKW
Dusseldorfer Strabe 40
Postfach 58 67
6236 Eschborn 1

World Council of Management
  (CIOS)
c/o NIVE
Van Alkemadelaan 700
2597 AW The Hague
Netherlands

Algeria

Institut National de la
  Productivité et du
  Développement Industriel
  INPED
125 bis rue Didouche
Mourad
Algiers

Argentina

Institute Para el Desarrollo de
  Empresarios en Argentina
Moreno 1850
P.piso
Buenos Aires

Australia

Australian Institute of
  Management
National Centre
Suite 18
65 Queens Road
Melbourne
Victoria

Australian Management
  (Graduates) Society
GPO Box 230
Sydney
NSW 2001

Austria

United Nations Industrial
  Development Organisation
  (UNIDO)
PO Box 300
A-1400 Vienna

Bahamas

Bahamas Institute of Commerce
Heasties Building
Robinson Road
PO Box N7917
Nassau

Belgium

Association International
  d'Etudiants en Sciences
  Economiques et Commerciales
  (AIESC)
Ave Adolphe Buyl 123
B-1050 Brussels

European Association of
  Management Training Centres
51 rue de la Concorde
Brussels 5

Management Centre Europe
4 Avenue de Arts
Brussels 4

European Institute for Advanced
  Studies in Management
Place Stephanie 20
B1050 Brussels

European Research Group on
  Management (ERGOM)
PrediKatrenberg 55
B3200 Kessel–10

Union Internationale Chretienne
  des Dirigeants D'Enterprise
  (UNIAPAC)
49 Avenue D'Auderghem
B-1040 Brussels

Botswana

Institute of Management
  Development
Botswana
PO Box 1357

Brazil

Instituto de Organizaçao
  Racional Do Trabalho
Praça Don Jose Gaspor 30
Sao Paulo

Canada

Canadian Institute of
  Management
2175 Sheppard Avenue East
Suite 110
Willowdale
Ontario
M2J 1W8

China

China Enterprise Management
  Association
Sanlihe
Fuxingmenwai
Beijing

Cyprus

Cyprus Productivity Centre
Ministry of Labour and Social
  Insurance
PO Box 536
Nicosia

Czechoslovakia

Czechoslovak Committee for
  Scientific Management
Director
Siroka 5
11001 Praha 1

Denmark

Danish Employers'
  Confederation
1503 Vestervoldgade 113
Copenhagen V

Egypt

Industrial Development Centre
  for Arab States
IDCAS
PO Box 1297
Cairo

Ethiopia

African Association for Public
  Administration and
  Management
PO Box 60087
Addis Ababa

Finland

Finnish Institute of Management
Director Kalevankatu 12
00100 Helsinki 10

France

Comité National De
  l'Organisation Française
3 Rue Cassette
Paris 6e

Association Française de
  Management (CNOF)
Director General
119 rue de Lille
75007 Paris

Centre International de
  Maintenance Industrielle (CIMI)
8 rue de l'Azin
41018 Blois Cedex

European Association for
  Personnel Management
72 rue St Louis en l'Ile
F-75004 Paris

European Federation of
  Management Consultants
3 rue Leon Bonnat
F-75016 Paris

European Industrial Research
  Management Association
  (EIRMA)
38 Cours Albert 1 er
75 Paris 8

Institut Européen
  d'Administration Des Affaires
  (INSEAD)
Boulevard de Constance
77305 Fontainebleau
Cedex

Institut Européen pour la
  Formation Professionnelle
28 Avenue Hoche
75008 Paris

Ghana

Ghana Institute of Management
  and Public Administration
Greenhill
PO Box 50
Achimota

Greece

Greek Management Association
27v Sophias Avenue
Athens

Greek Productivity Centre
28 Kapodistriou St
10682 Athens

Guyana

Guyana Institute of Management
c/o The Communications Officer
Bauxite Industry Development
  Corporation Ltd
71 Main and Murray Sts
PO Box 7
Georgetown

Hong Kong

Hong Kong Management
  Association
Management House 3rd Floor
26 Canal Road West

Hungary

National Management
  Development Centre
Konyves Kalman Korut 48–52
H-1476 Budapest VIII

India

All India Management
  Association
Management House Area
14 Institutional Area
Lodi Road
New Delhi 110 003

Indian Institute of Management
Diamond Harbour Road
PO Joka
via Calcutta

Institute of Business
  Management
MP Chapter Plot No 196
A Sector Indrapuri
Bhopal (MP)

Institute of Modern
  Management
30 Dr. Sundari Mohan Avenue
Calcutta 700014

National Productivity Council
Lodi Road
New Delhi 110 003

Indonesia

Akademi Keuangan Dan
Perbankan
Alanat
Dhalan Mugas No 1
Semarang

Ireland

Irish Management Institute
Director General
Sandyford Road
Dublin 14

Israel

Israel Institute of Productivity
Director
4 Henrietta Szold Street
Tel Aviv 61330

Israel Management Centre
PO Box 33033
Tel Aviv 61330

Italy

Ufficio Documentazione PRO
(IFAP)
Piazza della Reppublica 59
Roma 00185

Fondazione Giovanni Agnelli
Via Ormea 37
1–10125 Torino

Jamaica

Jamaican Institute of
Management
15 Hillcrest Avenue
Kingston

Japan

Foundation for Asian
Management Development
1704 Mori Building No 17
1–26–5 Toranoman
Minato-Ku
Tokyo 105

International Management
Association of Japan
Mori 10th Building
1–18–1 Toranoman
Minot Ku
Tokyo

Japan Management Association
3–11–22 Shiba Park
Minato-Ku
Tokyo 105

Jordan

Arab Organisation of
Administration Sciences
PO Box 17159
Amman

Kenya

Kenya Institute of Management
College House
Koinange Street
PO Box 43706
Nairobi

Malaysia

Malaysian Institute of
Management
227 Jalan Ampang
Kuala Lumpur 16 03

Malaysian Association of
  Productivity
133/A Jalan Gasing
Petaling Jaya
PO Box 557
Jalan Sultan

Mauritius

Maritius Institute of
  Management
Cerne House
13 La Chaussee
Port Louis

Mexico

Instituto Nacional De
  Administracion Publica
  (INAP)
Km 14.5 Carretera
Mexico-Toluca
Delegacion Cuajimalpa
CP 05110

Nepal

Institute of Management
Tribhuvan University
PO Box 1246
Kirtipur
Kathmandu

Netherlands

Netherlands Management
  Association (NIVE)
Managing Director
Van Alkemadelaan 700
2597 AW Den Hagg

New Zealand

New Zealand Institute of
  Management
Auckland Division
Management House
303 Manurau Road
Espom
Auckland Box 26–001

Nigeria

International Institute of
  Managerial Technology
PO Box 258
Owerri
Imo State

Nigerian Institute of
  Management
22 Alhaji Murtala Animashaun
Close
Off Adelabu Street
Surulere
PO Box 2557
Lagos

Centre for Management
  Development
Management Village
Shangisha
Off Lagos/Ibadan Expressway
Tollgate
PMB 21578 Ikeja
Lagos State

Norway

The Norwegian National
  Committee of Scientific
  Management
Wm. Thranesgt 98
Oslo 1

Pakistan

Pakistan Institute of
  Management
Clifton
Karachi – 6

Papua New Guinea

Papua New Guinea Institute of
  Management
PO Box 1010
Lae

Philippines

Asian Institute of Management
Eugenion Lopez Foundation
M C C PO Box 898
Makati
Rizal

Productivity and Development
  Centre
DAP Building
San Miguel Avenue
Ortigas
Pasig
Metro Manila

Poland

Management Organisation and
  Development Institute
UL Wawilska 56
02–067 Warsaw

Portugal

Centro De Formaçao Tecnica
  (LNETI)
Praca Principe Real 19
1200 Lisboa

Portuguese Management
  Association (APM) President
Av. Casal Ribeiro 48–6 Dt
1000 Lisboa

Sierra Leone

Sierra Leone Institute of
  Management
20 Lightfot Boston Street
PO Box 1426
Freetown

Singapore

Singapore Institute of
  Management
15 Scotts Road
04–02/13 Thong Teck Building
Singapore 0922

South Africa

The Manpower and
  Management Foundation of
  Southern Africa
Executive Director
PO Box 31993
Braamfontein

National Development and
Management Foundation of
South Africa
Management House
PO Box 31793
Braamfontein
Transvaal 2017

South African Institute of
Management
PO Box 56222
Pinegowrie 2123
Transvaal

Institute of Personnel
Management of South Africa
PO Box 31390
Braamfontein 2017

Soviet Union

Comecon Institute of
Management
Prospekt Kalinina 56
Moscow 121205 USSR

Spain

Circulo De Empresarios
Serrano Jower 5-2
28015 Madrid

Sweden

The Swedish Institute of
Management
Director General
PO Box 6501
11383 Stockholm

Switzerland

International Management
Development Institute
4 Chemin De Conches
Geneva CH-1231

European Management Forum
19 Chemin des Hauts-Crets
Cobgny
Geneva CH-1223

International Management
Institute Geneva
4 Chemin de Conches
Geneva CH-1231

Management Development
Institute (IMEDE)
PO Box 1059/MSF
Lausanne CH-1001

Taiwan

China Productivity Centre
11th Floor
201-26 Tun Hua North Road
Taipei
Taiwan 105 ROC

Tanzania

Eastern and Southern African
Management Institute Esami
PO Box 3030
Arusha

Thailand

Thailand Management
  Association
Samaggi Insurance Building
3rd Floor, Room No 5
308 Silom Road
Bangkok 10500

Trinidad

Management Development
  Centre Trinidad
PO Box 1301
Port of Spain

Tunisia

Industrial Center for Arab
  States
14 rue Yahia B Amor
Tunis

West Germany

Association for Work Study and
  Industrial Organisation (REFA)
Wittichstrasse 2
Postfach 4138
6100 Darmstadt

International Institute of
  Management
Science Center Berlin
Platz de Luftbrucke
1-3 D-1000 Berlin 42

Zambia

Zambia Federation of
  Employers
Permanent House
Cairo Road
Lusaka

Zimbabwe

Zimbabwe Institute of
  Management
7th Floor
Inslip House
Samara Machel Avenue
Harare
PO Box 3733

7 Reading list

(a) Books

Adair, J., Ayres R., Debenham, I. Y. and Despres, D. (eds), *A Handbook of Management Training Exercises*, British Association for Industrial and Commercial Education, London, 1978.

Argyle, M., *Social Interaction*, Methuen, London, 1969.

Argyris, C., *Intervention Theory and Method: A Behavioural Science View*, Addison-Wesley, London, 1970.

Ashton, D., Braiden, E. and Easterby-Smith, M., *Auditing Management Development*, Gower, Aldershot, 1980.

Beveridge, W. E., *The Interview in Staff Appraisal*, Allen and Unwin, London, 1975.

Bradford, L. P., *Making Meetings Work*, University Associates, La Jolla, 1976.

Bradford, L. P., Editor, *Group Development*, University Associates, San Diego, 1978.

Buchholz, S., *Creating the High performance team*, Wiley, NY, 1987.

Clarron, C. G., Eves, S. M. and Fenner, E. C., *Behaviour: A Guide for Managers*, Macmillan, London, 1976.

Cleland, D., *Engineering team management*, Van Nostrand Reinhold, 1986.

Cohen, A. M. and Smith, R. D., *The Critical Incident in Growth Groups*, University Associates, San Diego, 1976.

Crosby, R. P., *Planning Recommendations or Actions: A Team Development Guidebook*, University Associates, La Jolla, 1972.

Dingwall, R., *Tools for Team Development*, EMAS Publishing, Crawley, 1980.

Dyar, D. A. and Giles, W. J., *Improving Skills in Working with People: Interaction Analysis*, HMSO, London, 1974.

Dyer, W. F., *Teambuilding Issues and Alternatives*, Addison-Welsey, Massachusetts and London, 1977.

Eddy, W. B. *et al.*, *Behavioural Science and The Manager's Role*, University Associates, La Jolla, 1976.

Ends, E. J. and Page, C. W., *Organisational Teambuilding*, Winthrop, Cambridge, Massachusetts, 1977.

Food, Drink and Tobacco Industry Training Board, *Development at Work*, Food, Drink and Tobacco Industry Training Board, Gloucester, 1978.

Forbes Greene, S., *The Encyclopaedia of Icebreakers*, Applied Skills Press, San Diego, 1983.

Fordyce, J. K. and Weil, R., *Managing with People*, Addison-Wesley, London, 1971.

Francis, D. and Woodcock, M., *50 Activities for Self-Development*, Gower, Aldershot, 1982.

Guest, R., *Work teams and team building*, Pergamon Press, NY, 1986.

Harrison, R., 'Role negotiations', in *Readings in Organisational Psychology*, Prentice-Hall, London, 1974.

Honey, P., *Face to Face: A Practical Guide to Interactive Skills*, 2nd edition, Gower, Aldershot, 1988.

James, M. and Jongeward, D., *Born to Win*, Addison-Wesley, London, 1973.

Jones, J. E. and Pfeiffer, J. W., *Handbooks of Structured Experiences*, University Associates, La Jolla.

Jones, J. E. and Pfeiffer, J. W., *Instrumentation in Human Relations Training*, University Associates, San Diego, 1976.

Jones, J. E. and Woodcock, M., *Manual of Management Development*, Gower, Aldershot, 1985.

Kilcourse, T., *Management Team Development: A Problem-centred technique*, M. C. B. Publications, 1984.

Lawrence, P. R. and Lorsch, J. W., *Developing Organisations: Diagnosis and Action*, Addison-Wesley, London, 1969.

Lewis, R., Paine, N. and Stevenson, A., *Team working – a guide to management development groups*, National Extension College, Cambridge, 1985.

Lievegoed, B. C. J., *The Developing Organisation*, Tavistock,

London, 1973.
Lippitt, G. L., *Visualising Change*, University Associates, La Jolla, 1976.
Lippitt, G. L., This, L. E. and Bidwell, R. G., *Optimising Human Resources: Readings in Individual and Organisational Development*, Addison-Wesley, London, 1971.
Lloyd, P. C., *Creating a Management Team to Achieve Specific Results*, Indust. and Commercial Techniques, 1974.
McGregor, D., *The Human Side of Enterprise*, McGraw-Hill, Maidenhead, 1960.
Maddux, R., *Team building an exercise in leadership*, Crisp Publications, Los Altos, 1986.
Maier, N. F., *The Appraisal Interview: Three Basic Approaches*, University Associates, La Jolla, 1976.
Margerison, C. J., *Managing Effective Work Groups*, McGraw-Hill, Maidenhead, 1973.
Merry, U. and Allerhand, M., *Developing Teams and Organisations*, Addison-Wesley, London, 1977.
Nichol, B., *The team development process for health service administrators*, University of Manchester, 1981.
Pfeiffer, J. W. and Jones, J. E., Annual Handbooks for Group Facilitators, 1972, 1973, 1974, 1975, 1976, 1977, 1978, 1979, 1980, 1981, 1982, 1983, 1984, 1985, 1986, 1987, 1988, University Associates, La Jolla.
Pfeiffer, J. W. and Heslin, R., *Instrumentation in Human Relations Training*, University Associates, La Jolla, 1972.
Rackham, N. and Morgan, T., *Behaviour Analysis in Training*, McGraw-Hill, Maidenhead, 1977.
Rackham, N., Honey, P. and Colbert, M., *Developing Interactive Skills*, Wellens Publishing, Guilsborough, 1971.
Reddin, W. J., *Effective Management by Objectives*, Management Publications Ltd., London, 1971.
Revans, R. W., *Developing Effective Managers: A New Approach to Business Education*, Longman, Harlow, 1971.
Rimler, G., Small Business: *Developing the Winning Management Team*, Amer. Management Assoc., 1980.
Roberts, T., *Developing Effective Managers*, Institute of Personnel Management, London, 1974.
Schein, E., *Process Consultation*, Addison-Wesley, London, 1969.
Schein, E., *Organisational Psychology*, Prentice-Hall, London, 1970.
Schindler-Rainman, E., Lippitt, R. and Cole, J., *Taking your*

Meetings out of the Doldrums, University Associates, La Jolla, 1977.

Singer, E. J., *Effective Management Coaching*, Institute of Personnel Management, London, 1974. ·

Spartz, D., *Management vitality the team approach*, Society of Manufacturing Engineers, Publications/Marketing Services Division, Dearborn, Mich., 1984.

Sperry, L. and Hess, L. R., *Contact Counselling: Communication Skills for People in Organisations*, Addison-Wesley, London, 1974.

Urwick Orr and Partners and Clothing and Allied Products Industry Training Board, Improving Management Performance – Summary of five case studies, 1978.

Woodcock, M. and Francis, D., *Unblocking Your Organisation*, University Associates, San Diego, 1975.

Woodcock, M. and Francis, D., *Organisation Development through Teambuilding*, Gower, Aldershot, 1981.

Woodcock, M. and Francis, D., *The Unblocked Manager*, Gower, Aldershot, 1982.

Wynn, R., *Team Management: Leadership by Consensus*, Merrill, 1984.

(b) Articles

Jenks, J. and Kelly, J., Keys to Effective Teambuilding, in *Management (NZ)*, Sept. 1987, pp 31, 34.

Jones, J. E., Dealing with Disruptive Individuals in Meetings, in *The 1980 Annual Handbook for Group Facilitators*, University Associates, San Diego, 1980.

Jones, J. E. and Woodcock, M., Logistical Planning for Management Development Courses, in *Manual of Management Development*, Gower, Aldershot, 1985.

Mahoney, F. X., Team Development: How to Select the Appropriate Approach, *Personnel*, Nov.–Dec. 1981, pp 21–38.

Mahoney, F. X., Team Development: its role at the Workplace, in *Personnel*, Sept.–Oct. 1982, pp. 52–59.

Margerison, C. and McCann, R., High Performing Managerial Teams, in *Leadership and Organisation Development Journal*, vol. 5, no. 5, 1984, pp. 9–13.

Maude, B., Training in Team-Building, *Industrial and Commercial Training*, vol 12, no. 11, Nov. 1980, pp 460–462.

Murphy, E. and Price, C., Organisation Development in British Telecom, in *Leadership and Organisation Development Journal*, vol. 8, no. 2, 1987, pp v–viii.

Oliver, J. and Langford, J., Safety in Team Building – The Contracting Process, in *Industrial and Commercial Training*, vol. 19, no. 5, Sept.–Oct. 1987, pp 3–5.

Pfeiffer, J. W. and Jones, J. E., Design Considerations in Laboratory Education, in *The 1973 Annual Handbook for Group Facilitators*, University Associates, San Diego, 1973.

Rigby, J. M., The Challenge of Multinational Team Development, in *Journal of Management Development*, vol. 6, no. 3, 1987, pp 65–72.

Smith, B. and Theaker, W., Building Teams and Managing Change in a Local Government Authority, in *Industrial and Commercial Training*, vol. 19, no. 1, Jan.–Feb. 1987, pp 14–21.

Stewart, V. and Stewart, A., Good Housekeeping for Internal Courses, in *Managing the Manager's Growth,* Gower, Aldershot, 1978.

Wainwright, D., The Arrival of Team Building, in *Training*, vol. 6, no. 6, Aug. 1980, pp 8–9.

8 Instruments, training packages and films

1 *Team Development Inventory*, Trainers' Package. John E. Jones, San Diego, California, University Associates.

The Team Development Inventory is an instrument designed to help members of a work group clarify their perceptions of each other so that they can improve their interpersonal relations and their teamwork. The TDI trainers' package includes a set of ten instruments, ten handouts and a Facilitator's Guide

2 *The structured experience kit.* J. William Pfeiffer and John E. Jones Editors, San Diego, California, University Associates.

The kit contains 400 different structured experiences which the trainer can easily locate to give learning designs, many of which are suitable for Team Development.

3 *The Jones–Mohr listening test.* John E. Jones and Lawrence Mohr, San Diego, California, University Associates.

The pack of cassette, test forms and a Facilitator's guide provides feedback or listening accuracy, motives participants to work on their listening skills and demonstrates the need for listening improvement in teams.

4 *Employee and team development.* Lawrence N. Solomon and Betty Berzon, San Diego, California, University Associates.

Four cassettes and a facilitator's guide focusing on the basic interpersonal skills required in the work environment.

9 Training journals

TITLE	PUBLISHER	ADDRESS
Australia		
Training and Development in Australia	Australian Institute of Training and Development	PO Box 1011 Lalor Victoria 3075
Canada		
Canadian Vocational Journal	Canadian Vocational Association	PO Box 3435 Station "D" Ottowa Ontario KLP 614
European		
C E D E F O P News	European Centre for the Development of Vocational Training	Bundesallee 22 D-1000 Berlin 15
France		
Enterprises Formation	Association Nationale pour la Formation Professionnelle des Adults	13 Place de Villiers 93108 Montreuil

TITLE	PUBLISHER	ADDRESS
France cont.		
Journal de la Formation Continue		2 rue d'Amsterdam 75009 Paris
West Germany		
Bulletin A I O S P	International Association for Educational & Vocational Guidance	c/o Friedrichstrasse D-1000 Berlin 61
Hong Kong		
Vocational Training News	Vocational Training Council	15 Floor, Harbour Centre 25 Harbour Road Wanchai
India		
Indian Journal of Training and Development	Indian Society for Training & Development	B41 Institutional Area South of IIT New Delhi 110016
Italy		
Formazione e Lavoro	Ente Nazionale A C L I Istruzione Professionale	Via Giuseppe Marcora 18/20 00153-Rome
Japan		
Industrial Training	Japan Industrial & Vocational Training Association	Nihon Sangyo Kunren Kyokai 6th Floor Minamizuka Building 2–17–3 Shibuya Tokyo 150

TITLE	PUBLISHER	ADDRESS

South Africa

| *Journal for Technical and Vocational Education in South Africa* | South African Association for Technical & Vocational Education | c/o Technician Witwatersrand PO Box 3293 Johannesburg 200 |

United Kingdom

CBI Education and Training Bulletin	Confederation of British Industry	103 New Oxford Street London WC1A 1DU
Training Digest	John Chittock	37 Gower Street London WC1E 6HH
Training Officer	Marylebone Press Ltd	Lloyd's House 18 Lloyd's St Manchester M2 5WA

United States

Vocational Training	Capitol Publications Inc	1300 N 17th Street Arlington VA 22209
Training	Lakewood Publications Inc	50 S 9th Street Minneapolis MN 55402
Bulletin on Training	The Bureau of National Affairs Inc	1231 25th Street NW Washington DC 20037
Employment and Training Reporter	The Bureau of National Affairs Inc	1231 25th Street NW Washington DC 20037
Practical Supervision	Professional Training Associates Inc	212 Commerce Boulevard Round Rock TX 78664
Professional Trainer	McGraw-Hill Training Systems	Box 641, Del Mar CA 92014
Training and Development Alert	Advanced Personnel Systems	Box 1438 Roseville CA 95661

TITLE	PUBLISHER	ADDRESS
United States cont.		
Training and Development Journal	American Society for Training & Development	1630 Duke Street No 13332 Alexandria VA 22314
Training Today	American Society for Training & Development	Chicagoland Chapter 203 N Wabash Avenue Ste 2210 Chicago IL 60601
Federal Trainer	US Office of Personnel Management	Training Resources Management Division-W E D 7230 Washington DC 20044
Training News	Weingarten Publications Inc	38 Chauncey Street Boston MA 02111
Training Trends	TPC Training Systems	1301 S Grove Avenue Barrington IL 60010
Journal of Vocational Education Research	American Vocational Education Research Association	c/o Wesley E Budke National Center for Research in Vocational Education Ohio State University 1960 Kenny Road Columbus OH 43210

10 Business schools around the world

Business schools offer post-graduate degree or equivalent courses in Management or Business. As with Management Institutes the list is divided into

UK
USA
Rest of the World

BUSINESS SCHOOLS UK

Ashridge Management College
Berkhamsted
Hertfordshire

University of Aston
Management Centre
Nelson Building
Gosta Green
Birmingham 54

University of Bath School of
Management
Claverton Down
Bath
BA2 7AY

Queen's University of Belfast
Department of Business Studies
Belfast
Northern Ireland

University of Bradford
Management Centre
Emm Lane
Bradford
West Yorkshire
BD9 4JL

City University Business School
Frobisher Crescent
Barbican Centre
London
EC2Y 8HB

Cranfield Institute of
  Technology
Cranfield School of
  Management
Cranfield
Beds
MK43 0AL

Durham University Business
  School
Mill Lane
Durham
DH13 LB

University of Edinburgh
Scottish Business School
Department of Business Studies
William Robertson Building
50 George Square
Edinburgh
EH8 9JY

University of Glasgow
Division of the Scottish Business
  School
Glasgow

Henley The Management
  College
Greenlands
Henley-on-Thames
Oxon
RG9 3AU

University of Hull
Department of Management
  Systems and Sciences
Hull
HU6X 7RX

The International Management
  Centre from Buckingham
Castle Street
Buckingham
Buckinghamshire
MK18 1BJ

University of Lancaster
Gillow House
Bailrigg
Lancaster
LA1 4YX

University of Leeds
Department of Management
  Studies
Leeds
LS2 9JT

London Graduate School of
  Business Studies
Sussex Place
Regent's Park
London NW1 4SA

London School of Economics
Houghton Street
London
WC2A 2AE

University of London
Imperial College
Management Science
  Department
London
SW7 2BX

Loughborough University of
Technology
Department of Management
Studies
Loughborough
Leicestershire
LE11 3TU

University of Manchester
Manchester Business School
Booth Street West
Manchester
M15 6PB

University of Manchester
Institute of Science and
Technology
Department of Management
Science
PO Box 88
Sackville St
Manchester
M60 1QD

University of Oxford
Templeton College
Oxford Centre for Management
Studies
Kennington Road
Kennington
Oxford
OX1 5NY

University of Salford
Department of Business and
Administration
Salford
M5 4WT

University of Sheffield
Division of Economic Studies
Sheffield
S10 2TN

University of Strathclyde
Business School
130 Rottenrow
Glasgow
G4 0GE

University of Wales Institute of
Science and Technology
2 Museum Place
Cardiff
CF1 3BG

University of Warwick
School of Industrial and
Business Studies
Coventry
Warwickshire
CV4 7AL

BUSINESS SCHOOLS USA

University of California
Berkeley
Graduate School of Business
Administration
350 Barrows Hall
Berkeley
CA 94720

University of California Los
Angeles
UCLA Graduate School of
Management
405 Hilgard Avenue
Los Angeles
CA 90024

Carnegie-Mellon University
Schenley Park
Pittsburgh
Pennsylvania

University of Chicago
Graduate School of Business
1101 E.58th Street
Chicago
Illinois 60637

Columbia University
Graduate School of Business
105 Uris Hall
New York
NY 10027

Cornell University
Graduate School of Business
  and Public Administration
Ithaca
NY 14853

Dartmouth College
Amos Tuck School of Business
  Administration
Hanover
New Hampshire
03755

Harvard University
Graduate School of Business
  Administration
Boston
Massachusetts

University of Illinois
Department of Business
  Administration
219 Commerce West
Urbana
Illinois 61801

Indiana University
Bloomington
Indiana 47405

University of Kansas
202 Summerfield Hall
Lawrence
Kansas

Massachusetts Institute of
  Technology
Sloan School of Management
Cambridge
Massachusetts

University of Michigan
Graduate School of Business
  Administration
Ann Arbor
Michigan

New York University
Graduate School of Business
  Administration
100 Trinity Place
New York City
NY 10006

J.L. Kellogg Graduate School of
  Management
Northwestern University
Leverone Hall
Evanston
Illinois 60201

Pace University
Graduate School of Business
Pace Plaza
New York
NY 10038

University of Pennsylvania
Wharton Graduate Division
The Wharton School
102 Vance Hall CS
PA 19104

University of Pittsburgh
Graduate School of Business
Pittsburgh
PA 15260

University of Southern
  California
Graduate School of Business
University Park
Los Angeles
CA 90007

Stanford University
Graduate School of Business
Stanford
CA 94305

University of Virginia
The Colgate Darden
  Graduate School of Business
Administration
Box 6550
Charlottesville
VA 22906

BUSINESS SCHOOLS REST OF THE WORLD

Australia

University of Melbourne
Graduate School of Business
  Administration
Parkville
Victoria 3052

University of New South Wales
Australian School of
  Management
P.O. Box 1
Kensington
Sydney 2033

Belgium

Catholic University of Leuven
Department of Applied
  Economic Sciences
Dekenstraat 2
B-3000 Leuven

Université Catholique De
  Louvain
Institut d'Administration et de
  Gestion
Avenue de l'Espinette 16
B1348
Louvain-la-Neuve

Canada

McGill University
1001 Sherbrooke St. W.
Montreal
Quebec
H3A 1G5

McMaster University
Faculty of Business
Hamilton
Ontario
L8S 4M4

Queen's University at Kingston
School of Business
Kingston
Ontario
K7L 3N6

University of Western Ontario
School of Business
  Administration
Ontario
London
N6A 3K7

Faculty of Administrative
  Studies
York University
4700 Keele St
Toronto
Ontario
M3J 1P3

France

Insead–European Institute of
  Business Administration
Boulevard de Constance
F-77305 Fontainebleau Cedex

South Africa

University of Cape Town
The Graduate School of
  Business
Private Bag
Rondebosch 7700
Cape Town

University of Witwatersrand
Graduate School of Business
  Administration
2 St Davids Place
Parktown
Johannesburg

Spain

Iese
University of Navarra
Avenida Pearson 21
Barcelona

Switzerland

Imede-Management
  Development Institute
23 Chemin de Bellerive
Lausanne CH-1007

IMI–International Management
  Institute
4 Chemin de Conches
Geneva CH-1231

11 Other useful organizations in the UK

These are listed because they have publications, undertake assignments, give advice, run courses or supply information on human relations/teambuilding topics.

BACIE
16 Park Crescent
Regent's Park
London
W1N 4AP

British Institute of Mangement
Management House
Parker Street
London
WC2B 5PT

British Institute of Management
Cottingham Road
Corby
Northants
NN17 1TT

Confederation of British
  Industry
Tothill Street
London
SW1H 9LP

Department of Employment
St James's Square
London
SW1Y 4JB

Group Relations Training
  Association
56 Millbank Road
Darlington
Co. Durham
DL3 9NH

Industrial Society
48 Bryanston Square
London
W1H 8AH
and
Peter Runge House
3 Carlton House Terrace
London
SW1Y 5DG

Institute of Personnel
  Management
Central House
Upper Woburn Place
London
WC1H 0HX

Manpower Services Commission
Selkirk House
166 High Holborn
London WC1V 6PF

National Economic
  Development Office
Millbank Tower
Millbank
London
SW1P 4QX

Organisation Development
  Network
ODN Secretariat
Hatchetts
Butchers Lane
Preston
Hitchin
Hertfordshire
SG4 7TR